Little Sr   of the D   L

MW00987713

LITTLEST SUFFERING SOULS

Children Whose Short Lives
Point Us to Christ

LITTLEST SUFFERING SOULS

Children Whose Short Lives Point Us to Christ

AUSTIN RUSE

Foreword by Raymond Cardinal Burke

Austin Ruse

TAN Books
Charlotte, North Carolina

Cover design by Caroline Kiser

Cover image: *The Thanks Offering* (oil on canvas), Bouguereau, William-Adolphe (1867), Restored Traditions

Library of Congress Cataloging-in-Publication Data

Names: Ruse, Austin, author.
Title: The littlest suffering souls : children whose short lives point us to
     Christ / Austin Ruse ; foreword by Raymond Cardinal Burke.
Description: Charlotte : TAN Books, 2017.
Identifiers: LCCN 2016057316| ISBN 9781505108392 (hardcover) |
     ISBN 9781505108415 (epub)
Subjects: LCSH: Catholic children--Biography. | Suffering--Religious
     aspects--Catholic Church. | Catholic children--Death.
Classification: LCC BX4669 .R87 2017 | DDC 282.092/2--dc23
LC record available at https://lccn.loc.gov/2016057316

Published in the United States by
TAN Books
P. O. Box 410487
Charlotte, NC 28241
www.TANBooks.com

For my wife, Cathy,
and our daughters, Lucy and Gianna-Marie

CONTENTS

FOREWORD

THE mystery of suffering is one of the greatest questions of human life in our world. In our completely secularized age which has lost its awareness of the goodness and dignity of every human life, created in the image of God, the temptation is great to regard as meaningless the lives of those whose existence is marked by chronic and incurable sufferings. At the same time, the suffering of the innocent is for many people a source of difficulty and objection to the Christian faith.

Pope St. John Paul II, in his apostolic letter *Salvifici doloris*, "On the Christian Meaning of Human Suffering," issued on February 11, 1984, reflected on how the Gospel of Jesus Christ illuminates the mystery of suffering. Reflecting on St. Paul's teaching on the Cross, St. John Paul II wrote: "The Cross of Christ throws salvific light, in a most penetrating way, on man's life and in particular on his suffering. For through faith the Cross reaches man together with the Resurrection: the mystery of the Passion is contained in the Paschal Mystery."[1] The Pope went on to speak of the "Gospel of Suffering," which has been handed on in the Church. Referring to the example of the saints, he pointed out that "[d]own through the centuries and generations it has been seen that in suffering there is concealed

---

1   Pope St. John Paul II, Apostolic Letter *Salvifici doloris*, 11 February 1984, no. 21.

a particular power that draws a person interiorly close to Christ, a special grace."[2]

St. John Paul II explained how the Christian's suffering is transformed by the knowledge that human suffering can share in the work of Christ's Redemption:

> Faith in sharing in the suffering of Christ brings with it the interior certainty that the suffering person "completes what is lacking in Christ's afflictions"; the certainty that in the spiritual dimension of the work of Redemption he is serving, like Christ, the salvation of his brothers and sisters. Therefore he is carrying out an irreplaceable service. In the Body of Christ, which is ceaselessly born of the Cross of the Redeemer, it is precisely suffering permeated by the spirit of Christ's sacrifice that is the irreplaceable mediator and author of the good things which are indispensable for the world's salvation. It is suffering, more than anything else, which clears the way for the grace which transforms human souls.[3]

Pope St. John Paul II's teaching on the Christian meaning of suffering was expressed not only in his papal Magisterium, but also in the example of his life. Throughout the final years of his pontificate, the saintly pontiff continued to fulfill a demanding schedule of appointments and events, even as his physical suffering and weakness were ever more vividly apparent. Despite the suggestions of some that someone in such a debilitating condition could not serve as pastor of the universal Church, Pope St. John Paul II persevered in his exercise of the Petrine ministry, and gave an example to the world of the redemptive good of suffering embraced in union with the Cross of Christ.

The truth of redemptive suffering, united to the Cross of Christ, is seen in a most dramatic way in the lives of those who, at a very young age, are faced with terrible

---

2 Ibid., no. 26.
3 Ibid., no. 27; cf. Colossians 1:24.

diseases. The present work narrates the lives of three children who, in recent times, bore witness with their lives to the Christian meaning of human suffering. In contemplating the joyful spirit with which these children embraced the chronic sufferings that marked their short lives, we see how Christ, ever alive for us in the Church, poured into the hearts of these children the love of His glorious pierced Heart, enabling them to bear their sufferings with supernatural courage and charity.

In seeing the great courage and love displayed by these children in their acceptance of suffering, we see how God makes use of those whom the world considers weakest and most insignificant in order to bring about the marvels of His grace. We are thus reminded of the important truth taught by St. Thérèse of the Child Jesus and the Holy Face, Virgin and Doctor of the Church, in her teaching on the "Little Way" of spiritual childhood:

> You know that I have always wanted to be a Saint; but compared with real Saints, I know perfectly well that I am no more like them than a grain of sand trodden beneath the feet of passers-by is like a mountain with its summit lost in the clouds. . . . I searched the Scriptures for some hint of my desired *elevator*, until I came upon these words from the lips of Eternal Wisdom: *"Whosoever is a little one, let him come to Me"* (Prv 9:4). . . . *Your arms, My Jesus, are the elevator* which will take me up to Heaven. There is no need for me to grow up; on the contrary, I must stay little, and become more and more so.[4]

The children whose lives are recounted in this volume, precisely in their littleness, were lifted up by Christ to

---

4 St. Thérèse of the Child Jesus and the Holy Face, *The Story of a Soul*, trans. Michael Day, C.O. (Rockford, Illinois: TAN Books, 1997), pp. 140-41.

become examples of holiness and instruments of God's grace for those who knew them.

Reflecting on the goodness of redemptive suffering in the lives of the littlest members of Christ's Mystical Body, we recognize ever more clearly the truth about the goodness and dignity of every human life, created in the image of God. At the same time, the example of these children, and of all the little souls who, through the Christian centuries, have suffered in union with Christ, demonstrates the profound error and evil of the "culture of death" which views as meaningless the lives of children who suffer from debilitating illnesses, and which seeks to eliminate them through abortion and euthanasia.

It is my hope that in reading the lives of the "littlest suffering souls" we may all grow in appreciation of the profound truth of the redemptive good of human suffering, and may be inspired to an ever-greater confidence in the grace of God to sustain us in our own sufferings, whatever they may be. May our reflection on the redemptive suffering of these littlest souls also lead us to a greater reverence and love for the lives of all of our brothers and sisters in Christ, especially those who are most vulnerable and threatened in our secularized society. May Our Lady of Guadalupe, who appeared to St. Juan Diego in order to make known to all peoples the compassion of her maternal heart, help us to perceive more clearly the goodness of each human life, created in the image of God, and to care more effectively for all of our brothers and sisters without limit or boundary.

RAYMOND LEO CARDINAL BURKE
Vigil of Christmas, December 24, 2016

ACKNOWLEDGMENTS

IN telling the stories of Little Nellie, Mary Ann Long, and Antonietta Meo, I relied on the fine work of others, work that I would like to acknowledge. Much of Ellen Orgon's story comes from a book by anonymous authors called *The Life of Little Nellie of Holy God*, published by TAN Books and used with their permission.

Mary Ann Long's story was told by unnamed authors at the Dominican Nuns of Our Lady of Perpetual Help Home in Atlanta, Georgia. The edition upon which I relied provides no other information than that, but it is still possible to obtain used copies online. The quotes from Flannery O'Connor come from her introduction to the volume in my possession.

Venerable Antonietta Meo's cause for canonization proceeds apace in Rome. In researching the outline of her story, I relied on a very engaging article by the writer Stefania Falasca in the journal *30 Days*, which has ceased publication. The story can be accessed online, however. Nennolina's letters are available online at *www.john114. org*. No other information is provided at the site, but her letters make for incredibly moving reading. They, too, are highly recommended.

INTRODUCTION

MY wife, my two little girls, and I prayed for a sick boy from Northern Virginia named Brendan Kelly almost every night for years. We did not know him, though I knew his father, Frank, casually from public policy circles in Washington, DC. The Kellys were among the many mission-oriented families of St. Catherine of Siena Church in Great Falls, Virginia and the Siena Academy Montessori School my daughters attend.

Brendan had Down syndrome and suffered from leukemia, something he had battled on and off since he was a little boy. And so we prayed for Brendan Kelly, though we did not know him; indeed, we had never met him.

Brendan died at the age of sixteen. We attended his wake, which was a revelation. The line of people waiting to visit with, however briefly, and to comfort Frank and Maura Kelly, Brendan's sister, Molly, and his brother, Joe, was immense. It snaked from the altar back down the main aisle and out the front door and stayed that way for hours. The line moved slowly as each and every one wanted to stay and comfort Brendan's family. The funeral Mass was packed and included a wide range of people—high school boys and girls, defense industry mavens, government officials, locals—all of whom had been somehow affected by this boy.

We knew Margaret Leo, a little girl in a wheelchair all bent over on one side yet always smiling. I confess I did

not know her well. It is hard to break through the barrier
we erect in our minds about someone in a wheelchair. I
knew her father very well. Leonard Leo runs the Federalist Society in Washington, DC and is, therefore, a major
player in many important battles, including those for the
Supreme Court.

When Margaret died, it was expected in some ways and
yet still a surprise if that makes sense. I did not attend the
wake or the funeral at St. Thomas More Cathedral, but my
friend Patrick Fagan did, and he was quite simply stunned
and overwhelmed. The Cathedral was packed, and the reverence surrounding the memory of that little girl with spina
bifida moved Pat nearly beyond words. He kept her prayer
card and began a devotion to her that continues to this day.
Pat said the stories told that day were both simple and profound and that Margaret was assuredly a saint.

I knew Audrey's family for years: Lillian, an American
from Chicago with connections to Washington, DC and
Northern Virginia, and her husband, Jerome, a Frenchman
born in Paris and raised on Reunion Island east of Mada-
gascar. They live near Paris, but through our involvement
in Catholic apostolates, I have had occasion to work with
them both. I knew them for many years and they never told
me about Audrey, their daughter who suffered from leukemia and died at seven. Someone pressed a book into my
hands—a book about Audrey, her suffering, her faith, and
how she had drawn many to the faith or closer to it, including Liliane and Jerome themselves and their other children,
three of whom eventually entered religious life.

And so, being a writer, a series of columns came to
mind, a series about these children and what they suffered,

but more than that, who they were and how they affected their families, friends, and even strangers by their preter-natural—indeed their supernatural—acceptance of and approach to their maladies: all for the love of Christ and His Church.

The columns were published by my friend Dr. Robert Royal at his very fine website *The Catholic Thing (www. thecatholicthing.org)*. The response was quite remarkable. Dozens of requests came in from around the world for cop-ies of their prayer cards. Stories flooded in about children who lived similar lives.

And so the idea for a book began to jell. It seemed to me that these stories needed to be told to a wider audience. These children had stories to tell and lessons for us to learn, something that the good people at TAN Books also recog-nized immediately when I told them.

In the course of my research, I discovered that these three children were not the only examples of little suffering souls in the modern era but that others had come before them. I discovered Little Nellie of Holy God, the little girl who inspired Pope Pius X to change the rules for first Com-munion. I discovered Antonietta Meo, whose cause for canonization began in the twentieth century. I discovered Mary Ann Long when Robert Royal urged me to read an essay about her by Flannery O'Connor. And those are not all; there are others.

I also began to hear stories about children in persistent vegetative states who had miracles happening around them, unconscious children who had become the center of devo-tions. I heard stories about babies who lived the briefest of lives who had cults grow up around them.

While I do not reject these stories—not at all—I determined that the stories of Brendan, Margaret, and Audrey are of totally sentient children who knew what they were going through, knew they were sick or disabled, and accepted their suffering and offered it up for the love of God. In short, they knew what they were doing and what was happening to them and embarked upon a profoundly spiritual path as they undertook their own individual ways of the cross.

That is a remarkable thing and will be a leitmotif of this book. These children knew. Two of them knew they were dying. And even so, they offered it all to God for Him and His suffering on the Cross, for themselves, and for others. They knew.

Imagine that. What little pain it takes us to howl and hustle for the aspirin, or things even stronger, to dull the pain. How even the littlest inconveniences of the day can overwhelm us and upset us. How happiness can turn to sorrow over the most insignificant things.

It became clear to me that the focus of this book would be on children who suffered and who knew and understood what they were going through but who, at the same time, were also, in a very real sense, normal children of their time.

And how normal they were. They were not plaster saints. Brendan had a ribald, even an occasionally scatological sense of humor. After all he was a boy, a boy's boy. Margaret could grow frustrated if her mother or her brother did not pick up her crayon fast enough from the floor. While Audrey could be strict with her friends about modesty, she was nonetheless the life of the party.

We cannot and do not canonize these children. We cannot and do not beatify them. That is for the Church to do. It is inevitable, though, that local cults will grow up around those extraordinary witnesses to God's love in their corner of the world—those people, young or old, whom their neighbors think may be in heaven—and it is through these invocations, those favors asked and received, that the Church eventually comes to recognize saints in heaven. And those of us who knew them, and many who did not, believe this has already happened with each of the children you will read about here. But, again, ultimately it is for the Church to decide and we must be docile children of the Church . . . just as these children were.

This is their story, the story of three normal children each of whom possessed a simple yet supernatural understanding of the Faith and an intense love for Christ and His Church, three children who, through their maladies and sufferings, brought an intense life of faith to their families and led others to varying degrees of belief and practice.

We should all be more like *The Littlest Suffering Souls*.

LITTLE SUFFERING
SOULS IN HISTORY

S TORIES of children offering their suffering-unto-death to a loving God and bringing others closer to Him are not new. The story of the little suffering souls fits into a narrative as old as the Church herself. These stories are an important part of our patrimony. How else are we to view the stories of St. Agnes, St. Lucy, and the other child martyrs throughout history?

Their stories must be numerous, though largely hidden from us. Canonized saints throughout history have tended to come from the ranks of the clergy and other religious partly because of a common belief in the Church—lately being corrected through a new emphasis on the universal call to holiness—that spiritual excellence, true holiness, is accessible only to the ordained and consecrated. Moreover, upon dying, the most holy religious have built-in teams to support and promote their cause for canonization. Laymen don't. Children certainly don't.

By definition, children cannot be ordained or consecrated, nor do they live big, broad lives with large followings. They are known only to a few: their families, a few friends, doctors and nurses.

History has recorded, however, the stories of children who undoubtedly did scale the heights of sanctity—and not just the martyrs mentioned in the Holy Mass. However, for well into the twentieth century, except for martyrs, the Church declined to consider children for canonization because it was believed they could not knowingly live the virtues heroically. Since 1981, however, that practice has been modified, as the Congregation for the Causes of Saints is now considering non-martyred children as candidates for sainthood.

Stories of children in the modern age living lives of heroic virtue abound. Better known examples include Blesseds Jacinta and Francisco of the Fatima apparitions, both of whom suffered greatly during the persecution they experienced as a result of the apparitions and later.

They were castigated and threatened by many for the story they told. And then they both got terribly sick with the influenza that took millions of lives in those days. Their final suffering, which they offered for the conversion of sinners and to make reparation for offenses against the Immaculate Heart of Mary, was beyond the ken of almost any adult. They have been beatified, and they very well may become the first non-martyr children raised to the altars by Holy Mother Church. Their stories are well known and will become even more so in this the centennial of the apparitions of Fatima.

Less well known, however, are Little Nellie of Holy God, Venerable Antonietta Meo, and Mary Ann Long.

2

LITTLE NELLIE OF HOLY GOD

IT is now a common practice for young children to receive Holy Communion. This was not always the case, however. It was Pope Saint Pius X who changed the practice of having Catholics wait until their early teens to receive; his inspiration for doing so came from a little girl who was born in Waterford, Ireland in 1903 and died in Cork five short years later, a little girl who has come to be known as Little Nellie of Holy God.

From an early age, Ellen Orgon showed precocious faith. At the age of two, walking to Mass with her soldier-father, she would "prattle all the way about Holy God. That is the way she always spoke about God, and I do not know where she could have learned it," said her father.

When her mother died, it was immediately apparent that her father could not care for five children, so the children were split up and sent to various convents. Nellie went to the Good Shepherd Sisters who soon discovered that the always-delicate Nellie suffered from a crooked spine and that she found it painful to simply sit up in a chair for very long.

But worse than that, when called upon to remove some beads that the all-too-normal three-year-old had swallowed, doctors discovered Little Nellie also had the sickness that had taken her mother: the dread disease

3

tuberculosis. From the moment of that diagnosis, Little Nellie had only eight months to live—eight months that have come to be known around the world, down through time, and into eternity. But she would live a beautiful life in those short eight months.

In the infirmary, Little Nellie made a life-long friend with her nurse, Miss Hall, whom she began to call her "Mudder."

"Holy God took my Mudder, but He has given me you to be my Mudder," Nellie said.

Her new Mudder loved Nellie deeply. She catechized Little Nellie, teaching her about the Infant of Prague—a statue of whom sat nearby on a small altar—and from that moment, Nellie developed a keen devotion to the Child Jesus, whom she called her "baby", often hugging and kissing the statue.

She once asked her friend Mary Long to play a tune on a tin whistle because the Baby Jesus was dancing for her, and He really was. In a kind of ecstasy, Nellie saw Him.

Nellie prayed a novena to the Infant of Prague, asking Him for healing, and for a time, she was at least healed enough to walk in the nearby garden. Inspired by Nellie's devotion to the Baby Jesus, the prioress once knelt on the floor near His statue and prayed to Him for a bakehouse so the nuns could bake their own bread rather than buy it. Within days, a check for several thousand dollars arrived marked "for a bake house."

Though her days were long and dreary, given to loneliness and pain, Nellie loved her Holy God. The nuns brought her flowers, and she exclaimed, "Isn't Holy God good to have made such lovely flowers for me." She eschewed fake plastic flowers. "They are too tiff. Bring me some of Holy God's own flowers." Dead flowers she called "dirty" and insisted that holy statues be decorated only with real flowers.

The nuns came to know that Nellie had a supernatural devotion to Christ in the Holy Eucharist. One morning, she reproached her friend Mary Long for not attending Mass.

"You did not get Holy God this morning," Nellie said to Mary.

"How do you know, lovey?"

"No matter. I know you didn't get Holy God."

The next day, Mary opened and closed her door as if going to Mass and removed her shoes and moved around quietly. Later Little Nellie said to her, "You did not get Holy God this morning." Somehow Nellie knew.

Little Nellie had never been to exposition of the Blessed Sacrament before, yet when she was taken for the first time, she exclaimed, "Mudder, there He is. There is Holy God now," pointing to the monstrance. Somehow Nellie knew.

Clearly weak and weakening more by the day, the prioress informed the bishop that four-year-old Nellie Organ was in the home and very frail. The bishop was moved during Holy Mass that it was time to confirm the little girl. The prioress hurried to teach Little Nellie what she needed to know for Confirmation and to her surprise, discovered that Nellie knew everything already. When the bishop confirmed her, Nellie exclaimed, "I am now a soldier of Holy God."

As her life neared its end, Nellie experienced terrible pain. She was wasting away from the tuberculosis. At the same time, she developed a disease of the jaw, and her jawbone began literally falling apart. The odor was appalling. When in severest pain, Nellie would lie with her arms across her chest holding a crucifix. She would unite herself with the suffering of Our Lord on the Cross and say, "Poor Holy God. Oh, poor Holy God." When others sympathized with her for her suffering, she would say it was nothing compared to what Christ suffered for her on the Cross.

Even the other children knew there was something special about Little Nellie: that she had an understanding of the Faith that was beyond them, beyond even the adults.

There came a time when Little Nellie began to long for the Eucharist, which was not allowed for children so young at the time. Even so, one evening Nellie asked the prioress to bring her Holy God from Mass the next morning. When the prioress arrived without the Eucharist, Nellie spent the day in quiet sadness. She kept asking. Continually refused, she then began to ask the prioress and others to come to her immediately after Communion and kiss her on the lips so she could receive the Eucharist at least indirectly.

One day the nuns went on retreat, and they told the priest about Little Nellie and her desire to receive the Holy Eucharist. The priest quizzed her and found her knowledge of the Eucharist more than sufficient, so he wrote to the bishop. When the bishop's approval arrived, the priest rushed to Little Nellie who was overjoyed, "I will have Holy God in my heart. I will have Holy God in my heart."

The night before her first Communion, Little Nellie could not sleep. She kept begging to be taken downstairs.

When the time arrived, she received with profound recollection and stayed recollected all throughout the day; this attitude remained with her for the rest of her short life and through the reception, they say, of thirty-two more Eucharists. She often had to receive in her bed, as she was too weak to move.

Her preparation for the Holy Eucharist and her thanksgiving afterwards were much remarked upon. Some of the nuns would come simply to watch her as she entered a kind of ecstasy before and after. Even the bishop of Cork made mention of her heroic suffering. Though her first Holy Communion did away with the terrible smell of her deteriorating jaw, a miraculous occurrence in itself, the terrible pain remained. One priest noted, "Her days of torture glided into weeks of agony. . . ."

While in great pain herself, Little Nellie prayed for the suffering of others to end, and it often did. She prayed for illnesses to end, and they, too, did. All these petitions were granted to her as she herself lay dying.

Nellie Orgon, the little girl who loved her Holy God so much and had His name on her lips so often that it became part of her own name, said she would go to Him on His day, and so she did, passing into eternal life on Sunday, February 2, 1908. She was not yet four-and-a-half years old. Her body was later found to be incorrupt. Pope Saint Pius X requested a relic of Little Nellie and began a Court of Enquiry as a first step toward canonization. He died before this was realized, but before he died, he changed the rule regarding the age at which children may receive first Holy Communion and said Little Nellie was the reason he did so. Now, little children the world over could approach the Holy God just like Little Nellie.

3

VENERABLE ANTONIETTA MEO

"THERE will be saints among the children," said Pope Pius X as he changed the age for children to receive their first Holy Communion from twelve to seven.

Somehow as an answer to this prophesy, in 1936, not long before her death, six-year-old Antonietta Meo wrote, "Dear Jesus Eucharist, I am so very, very happy that you have come into my heart. Never leave my heart, stay for ever and ever with me. Jesus I love you so, I want to let myself go in your arms and do what you will with me. . . . O loving Jesus give me souls, give me a great many!"

This was her letter to Jesus shortly after she received her first Holy Communion and after cancer had led to the amputation of her leg. Three months later, on July 3, 1937, she would be dead of bone cancer.

She was one of those foreseen by Pius X. Antonietta Meo suffered massively from her cancer, but throughout her personal way of the cross, she enthusiastically praised God for her pain so that she could offer it to Him.

Antonietta was born on December 15, 1930 to a wealthy family in Rome within the parish of Santa Croce in Gerusalemme. Though the site is of great renown in the Church as the estate where St. Helen once lived and where she brought various artifacts, including relics of the True Cross, the church was not founded as a parish until the time of Pope St. Pius X in 1910.

The basilica is one of the "Seven Churches" that ancient pilgrims visited, a devotion that has been revived in recent years.

At the age of four, after her parents noticed a swelling of her knee, Nennolina—as she was affectionately known—was diagnosed with bone cancer. She suffered greatly for the rest of her life; that suffering including the amputation of her leg in April of 1936.

Her father asked her once if she was in great pain, and she replied, "Daddy, the pain is like fabric, the stronger it is, the more value it has." A nun listening nearby said, "If I had not heard this with my own ears, I would not have believed it."

Five months after doctors took her leg, Nennolina began dictating a trove of letters to Jesus, which she would place at the feet of a statue of the Baby Jesus near her bed. Her first letter began, "Dear Jesus, today I am going out and I'm going to tell them I want to make my First Communion at Christmas. Jesus come soon into my heart and I'll hug you very tight and kiss you. O Jesus, I want you to stay forever in my heart."

She also wrote, "My good Jesus, give me souls, give me a lot of them, I ask you willingly, I ask you so that you make them become good and so that they can come to you in Paradise." These are intentions that one would expect from someone far advanced in the interior life. And yet she was only six.

On the eve of her first Holy Communion, Nennolina wrote something her mother did not understand: "Dear Jesus, tomorrow when you are in my heart, pretend that my soul is an apple. And as there are pips in the apple, make it that there is a little cupboard in my soul. And since under the black skin of the pips there is the white seed, make it so that in the little cupboard there is your grace, like the white seed."

Her mother said, "But Antonietta, what are you saying? What's this inside that's inside? What does it mean?"

"Listen Mommy, let's say my soul is an apple. In the apple there are those little black things that are the seeds? Then inside the skin there's that white thing? Well, think of that as grace."

"But these things you've been telling me . . . the teacher at school took an apple to explain to you . . ."

"No, Mommy, the teacher didn't tell me, I thought it up myself. Jesus is seeing to it that this grace will always, always, be with me."

Little Antonietta was a great letter writer, although her letters were not always deliverable by mail. It is said she wrote more than one hundred letters to Jesus and others to Mary, God the Father, the Holy Spirit, one to St. Agnes, and one to St. Thérèse of the Child Jesus.

Her last letter is dated June 2. "Dear crucified Jesus, I love you and am so fond of you! I want to be with you on Calvary. Dear Jesus, tell God the Father that I love him, too. Dear Jesus, give me your strength for I need it to bear this pain that I offer for sinners." Her mother, who was writing it down, said her daughter was then overcome with coughing and vomiting, but she continued. "Dear Jesus, tell the Holy Spirit to enlighten me with love and to fill me with his seven gifts. Dear Jesus, tell Our Lady that I love her and want to be near her. Dear Jesus I want to tell you again how much I love you. My good Jesus, look after my spiritual father and grant him the necessary grace. Dear Jesus, look after my parents and Margherita. Your little girl sends you lots of kisses. . . ." At this point her mother became enraged at the poor girl's suffering, crumpled up the letter, and threw it in a drawer. It was not to stay there. It ended up in the hands of the pope.

It happened this way. Not long after her mother crumpled up that letter, the Meo family doctor asked a colleague to examine the girl. His colleague, a Dr. Milani, was also the pope's doctor. Dr. Milani was deeply impressed with Nennolina's patient suffering. Her father showed him the crumpled letter, and the doctor was so moved he asked if he could show it to the pope. The very next day, a Vatican car pulled up to the Meo house carrying Pope Pius XI's apostolic blessing.

Nennolina's suffering continued. At one point, fluid had to be drawn from her lungs. And then, with only local anesthetic, doctors cut out three of her ribs. Her mother said, "I cannot tell you how that poor tortured body suffered. Holding back my tears that day I said to her, 'Wait and see my darling . . . as soon as you're stronger we'll go on vacation, we'll go to the seaside . . . you love the seaside . . . you'll be able to swim, you know. . . .' She looked at me . . . and she sweetly said, 'Mommy, cheer up, be glad . . . I'll be gone from here in under ten days.'"

Her mother asked for her blessing. Nennolina made the Sign of the Cross on her own mother's forehead.

Little Antonietta, so young yet so wise in the ways of God, was right, and on July 3, 1937, she whispered, "Jesus, Mary . . . Mommy, Daddy," and passed away.

Within a few years, two biographies appeared. The priest who first published her letters wrote, "Behold the wonderful workings of God. The grace of God chooses souls where it will. That is the only explanation for the words, the playfulness, the attitudes, the life of Nennolina."

The Future Pope Paul VI, then substitute secretary of state wrote, "Truly the Lord *ludit in orbe terrarum* and, working through souls in the most mysterious ways, he grants to many, through the life of this child, not yet seven years old, the chance of penetrating the knowledge that is hidden from the proud and revealed to little ones."[1]

On December 17, 2007, Pope Benedict XVI declared her Venerable. He told her story to Italian youth three days later:

> Exactly three days ago, I decreed the recognition of her heroic virtues and I hope that her cause of beatification will soon be successfully concluded. What a shining example this little peer of yours left us! In her very short life - only six and a half years - Nennolina, a Roman child, showed special faith, hope and charity, and likewise the other Christian virtues. Although she was a frail little girl, she managed to give a strong and vigorous Gospel witness and left a deep mark on the diocesan Community of Rome. . . . Her life, so simple and at the same time so important, shows that holiness is for all ages: for

---

1 Stefania Falasca, "The little letters of 'Nennolina,'" 30Days (May 2010): http://www.30giorni.it/articoli_id_22702_13.htm.

children and for young people, for adults and for the elderly. Every season of our life can be a good time for deciding to love Jesus seriously and to follow him faithfully. In just a few years, Nennolina reached the peak of Christian perfection that we are all called to scale; she sped down the "highway" that leads to Jesus. Indeed, as you yourselves said, Jesus is the true "road" that leads us to the Father and to his and our definitive home, which is Paradise. You know that Antonia now lives in God and is close to you from Heaven: you feel her present among you, in your groups. Learn to know her and follow her example.[2]

If Nennolina is declared a saint, she would become the youngest non-martyr ever so-named by the Church.

---

2 Address of His Holiness Benedict XVI to the Children of Catholic Action, December 20, 2007.

4

MARY ANN LONG

THOUGH she never met Mary Ann Long, novelist Flannery O'Connor nonetheless described her as "an extraordinary rich girl." This even though she was born dirt poor, left by her family at a home for terminal patients, and lived her entire short life with an ugly and painful tumor that horribly disfigured her face and eventually killed her.

How did O'Connor come to know of this girl whom she had never met in person? The mother superior of the Hawthorne Dominicans of Atlanta, Georgia had written O'Connor asking her to write the life story of Mary Ann Long, and they sent along a photograph of the girl who had already passed away.

O'Connor declined to write the book, but she provided the introduction: "[The photograph] showed a little girl in her first Communion dress and veil. She was sitting on a bench, holding something I could not make out. Her small face was straight and bright on one side. The other was protuberant, the eye was bandaged, the nose and mouth crowded slightly out of place. The child looked out at her observer with an obvious happiness and composure. I continued to gaze at the picture long after I had thought to be finished with it."

O'Connor, so wise about grotesqueries, called Mary Ann's defect "plainly grotesque."

All we know about Mary Ann Long was written by the Hawthorne Dominicans in a book called *A Memoir of Mary Ann*. It should be noted that the Hawthorne Dominicans were founded by Rose Hawthorne, a convert and the daughter of the great American novelist Nathaniel Hawthorne who, himself, had once been accosted by a small child in a workhouse for children who was so grotesque Hawthorne could not tell the child's sex. Hawthorne held the physically repulsive child, and O'Connor drew a straight line from that moment to his daughter's conversion, her call to care for the indigent poor dying of cancer, and on to Mary Ann's life at the home.

Mary Ann Long was born to poor parents in 1946. She was brought by her parents to Our Lady of Perpetual Help Free Cancer Home in Atlanta when she was three years old after doctors in her native Louisville, Kentucky determined that the tumor on the left side of her face was a malignancy and that she had no more than six months to live. Her eye had already been removed, and she had undergone blood transfusions, radium, and all the other crude treatments available in the late 1940s.

Because she was terminal and there was nothing they could do for her, the doctors in Louisville said she had to leave the hospital. Her young mother, not well herself, exhausted with three other children, one of them a baby, and by grinding poverty, did not know what to do.

The doctors recommended the Catholic home 420 miles away in Atlanta, a proposal truly strange to this unchurched family in the Bible Belt. The father had his own objection; he had been raised in an institution and hated them. However, the sickly mother needed all her strength to care for the others, and if she became incapacitated, the whole family would be utterly shattered and, perhaps, all of the children scattered.

And so, to the Hawthorne Dominicans they went. It was not as if Mary Ann's parents did not want her or love her. They did. How could they not, especially from what we learn about her? She might have been misshapen, even grotesque, but she was sweet and kind and exuberant, attributes that made themselves known the minute she walked into the home and, though she had never seen such strangely dressed women, flew into the outstretched arms of Sister Veronica.

Mary Ann did not die in three months or three years. Indeed, she lived for nine more years in that home, and during that time, she became the very heart of both the nuns and their other patients.

Perhaps the characteristic and most striking thing about Mary Ann Long was her utter indifference to her own suffering, including indifference to her own repugnant facial features. They did not make her shy. They did not encumber her at all, nor did they frighten away others, because people were able to see past them immediately to the true beauty inside that remarkable girl. Such was the joy Mary Ann Long exuded.

A hint as to Mary Ann's exuberant personality is found in the following delightful anecdote. Though her parents were unchurched, they agreed to have her baptized. When

Monsignor Dodwell blew into her face, she blew back in his. She was only three after all.

Though the home, that now sits literally in the shadow of Turner Field where the Atlanta Braves play baseball, is a place where the sick come to die, it became for Mary Ann a field of a different sort, her lifelong mission field, Mary Ann Long's apostolate of happiness; she became the beloved of the nuns, the other patients, the doctors, outsiders, the man who worked the yard, a businessman who played Santa, and so many others enchanted by the little girl with the misshapen face. People brought her child-sized furniture. The mother superior broke down and let her have a dog, the ugliest of the litter, that Mary Ann called "Scrappy."

Mary Ann embraced the religious instruction at the home. The nuns taught her the catechism. She was taken through the chapel and taught the Stations of the Cross where she would murmur, "Oh, poor Jesus." At prayers she would say, "Jesus, I love with you with all my heart," though she pronounced "heart" as "got."

Once a visiting doctor was examining her face, and she told him, "When I get to heaven, I'll have two good eyes and I'll run all around heaven and be able to see everybody there at once." People would ask if she ever prayed for her face to be corrected. No, she said, "This is how God wants me."

Like all children, however, she had her fears. Physical darkness plagued her. She said to Sister Loretta, "You know, Sister, it must be nice up in heaven. All light, but down here, it's kind of dark isn't it?" The nun told her heaven is our true home but that our work for God begins on earth. "You mean we make it so bright and happy here that everyone will know what it'll be like in heaven," said the already wise little girl. Even in a place to die, Mary Ann determined she could make it a glimpse of heaven for others.

Grasping that concept in a way few adults do and taking it to heart, Mary Ann sought to do good to those around her. Her works of mercy abounded. For instance, she often took her meals at the side of patients who could not get out of bed. Thinking of those less fortunate than herself, she asked one of the sisters if they could send cookies to the poor children of Louisville. "They don't have any up there," she said.

Her solicitous care and concern for others was perhaps best exemplified by her relationship with a new girl at the home. One day a three-year-old named Ginny arrived, and for her brief life, she was Mary Ann's roommate. Ginny could not walk but could be propped on pillows and taken around in a stroller, which is what Mary Ann did. Ginny could be a "hard case," which made for some humorous exchanges between the two. One of the nuns heard the following conversation between the two sick girls:

"Do you love me, Ginny?"

"No."

"Do you love the Sisters?"

"No."

"Do you love the patients?"

"No."

"Don't you even love your Mama?"

"Yes."

When Ginny died, Mary Ann was sure she was in heaven, and she began immediately to pray for a new "baby" to take care of. She kept Ginny's picture in her dresser drawer for the rest of her life.

Mary Ann's religious sensibilities were profound, and she cried because she wanted to begin receiving the Holy Eucharist. They prepared her for an entire year. When they went to her room that morning, she was already up and on her knees. The nuns wrote, "Her recollected demeanor was an *exultet*. She whispered almost audibly her thanksgiving."

The world outside the Home was not as understanding of Mary Ann's disfigurement. In Louisville, during visits with her family, she encountered the shocked looks of others when they first saw her misshapen face. The children stared, and her mother even tried to get her to see a plastic surgeon, but Mary Ann demurred saying this was how God wanted her.

Whether through her example or her active evangelization, Mary Ann succeeded in an area in which many of us struggle mightily and often fail. She brought members of her own family to Catholicism. When her sister Sue came for summer visits, she would spend most of her time in the chapel praying. Mary Ann had been praying for years that her family would become Catholic. Her mother actually tried to take Sue to a Protestant church in Louisville, but Sue was stricken by the experience because she wanted to be a Catholic. Her mother took her to Mass from then on and allowed her to go to Catholic school and begin instruction in the Faith. Sue took her first Holy Communion in Mary Ann's presence in Atlanta.

In short order her sister Winnie joined the Church and then her sister Doris Marie.

One event toward the end of her life shows God's plan in the life of children like Mary Ann and how their lives are far from useless, even though they would be judged so by many in this age that does not understand the most basic truths about the human person. Mary Ann eventually began to fade, to weaken, and it was noticeable to all who knew her. Even more ominously, the tumor on her face began to grow.

For years Mary Ann had prayed for a little baby to take care of. Sister Loretta told her, "He will (answer this prayer) when it's time." The nun was afraid, though, because she knew that when all of Mary Ann's prayers had been answered, such as the conversion of her sisters, that God would take her from them. And then baby Stephanie arrived.

Stephanie was the seventh child born to a loving family. But immediately at her birth, the doctors said she would not live. Doctors said she should be left to die: "It is useless to itself and to everyone else."

The family priest urged them to take the child to the sisters and to Mary Ann who was immediately struck with guilt. She said to the child's mother, "I didn't pray for a baby to be sick, but I prayed if a baby was sick, it would come here."

The mother later said, "By the time we brought the baby to the Home, I had accepted my child's affliction; I had accepted the hurt it brought me, but I had not accepted the fact I had to give her up. Mary Ann's words opened my understanding. Stephanie was needed; she wasn't useless; this child with the bandaged face and heart full of love needed her. What did I know about God's purpose?

Besides, what was I doing feeling sorry for myself? God had given me a good husband, six beautiful children. The last child was probably the most special of them all, destined for something I knew nothing about. My whole attitude changed, and as the months passed and we came back frequently to see Stephanie, the hurt healed and was replaced by a quiet joyful gratitude for her. Not only did she bring happiness to Mary Ann but she brought it to all in the Home; to the young mothers who were coaxed to babysit; to the old ladies who adored her; and to the Sisters who tried their best to spoil her."

It was not long after the new baby's arrival that Mary Ann's final suffering began. On September 30, 1958 she woke up with a massive hemorrhage from her facial tumor. She joked about it.

Knowing the end was likely near, the sisters decided it was time to grant one of Mary Ann's most fervent wishes: to be initiated as a Third Order Dominican. In a solemn ceremony in the chapel, Mary Ann Long became Sister Loretta Dorothy.

The hemorrhages continued. Even so, perhaps knowing her time was short, Mary Ann received a parade of visitors and, though busy making clothes for Stephanie and terribly fatigued, she happily greeted them all, "making them feel their company was her greatest desire."

Mary Ann's decline was rapid. Within weeks an enormous growth appeared in her mouth, "a mouth already stretched beyond its full width so that it seemed impossible she could ever have a relaxed, comfortable moment." The stretching also caused it to itch terribly, but to scratch it would cause bleeding, so Mary Ann was made to wear gloves to bed. At various times, the Dominican sisters gathered around Mary Ann's bed and sang the Salve Regina, a custom of the Order performed for the dying. During one hemorrhage shortly before Christmas, Mary Ann held a candle and said over and over, "Jesus, I love you."

Christmas Mass was said that year in her room with her family present, including her mother and father. Mary Ann held on through Christmas and New Year's. By then she could no longer eat or drink and so lived on cracked ice. She liked orange drink poured over the ice, and a case was delivered by strangers.

One day a character seemingly out of a Flannery O'Connor story came to see her. A faith healer arrived and found his way to her room. "Did you know the Lord Jesus can heal you, Mary Ann?" he asked.

"I know he can."

"The Lord Jesus can heal you."

"I know the Lord Jesus can heal me. I know he can do anything. It doesn't make a bit of difference whether he heals me or not. That's his business." The young man went away "funny like", said Mary Ann. No wonder O'Connor, who so skillfully brought the southern religious landscape to life, was intrigued by this girl.

Eventually, the end came, and unable to eat or drink and bleeding constantly, Mary Ann died one night holding the rosary that she often used when she could not sleep.

The small chapel at the Home was packed with priests and nuns and friends for her Requiem Funeral Mass. The bishop was there, as was the abbot of the nearby Trappist monastery. In his sermon, the bishop said Mary Ann's life and death would not be understood by the rules of the world, which is a one-sided viewpoint. The world fails to take into account that the purpose of our lives is to know, love, and serve God and to prove our worthiness of eternal happiness with Him in heaven. The bishop said, "Almighty God disposes all things not only well but sweetly. Precious in the sight of the Lord is the death of his saints."

There are so many others to write about: children who died young, who suffered—often terribly—before they died, but had a supernatural understanding of the Faith. There is Blessed Montse Graces of Spain who committed her life to Christ at a young age and who died of leukemia at eighteen. There is Carlo Acutis, an Italian boy who also died of leukemia at fifteen and is the subject of a biography and whose cause for canonization has much popular support. There are so many more.

Mary Ann Long, however, is the perfect subject to provide us a segue into the story of three children: two from Fairfax County, Virginia and a third from Paris, France. One notices nothing overly dramatic in the life of Mary Ann Long, just a life lived constantly in the presence of God. But for the book by the sisters and their letter to Flannery O'Connor, her story might have never been known except to those who knew her, most of whom are now gone. And such is the case of the Littlest Suffering Souls—Brendan of Great Falls, Margaret of McLean, and Audrey of Paris—whom you will now meet.

5

BLESSED BE PAIN, SANCTIFIED BE PAIN

THE story of the Littlest Suffering Souls will not make sense without an understanding of the Catholic teaching on pain and suffering. One's understanding the teaching, however, does not guarantee agreement because, to many, the teaching is unique, unbelievable, even scandalous.

Pain and suffering are not exactly the same thing. Pain is when you bump your head on the cabinet door, when you bang your knee on the car door, when they jam a needle in your spine for a tap. Suffering is what you do with it. Suffering is related to the mind and the imagination. St. Thomas Aquinas said the imagination is the madman of the soul. What he meant was that suffering, whether from pain or insult or worry, can drive you mad. The person who wants to commit suicide out of fear of pain, real or imagined, is said to be well and truly suffering.

We live in a pain-obsessed age. Perhaps ironically, more books have been written about pain since we have learned to control it (for the most part) than in all the centuries when there was no such thing as aspirin, let alone more powerful pain relievers. The ancients chewed on leaves.

Put "pain" in the search bar at Amazon.com and more than one hundred pages of titles on the topic will appear. Most of the books do concern themselves with the physiological reasons that we hurt—our backs, shoulders, legs, hearts, and so on—but the greatest emphasis is often on how to prevent pain and how to control it. Modern man is obsessed with pain.

Imagine ancient man. You have to think he endured more pain than we do, given that he may have had only certain leafs to relieve it, and because of that, he probably did not think about it as much as we do. This is counterintuitive. We moderns have unprecedented resources with which to control pain, and so even slight discomfort sends us to the medicine cabinet, and yet still libraries could be filled with books on the subject. Ancient man had little to no ability to control or reduce pain; therefore, he did not think about it nearly as much as we do. There was nothing to think about or obsess over.

He certainly knew horrific pain. Consider his experience of surgery. Among the earliest surgeries in ancient Egypt was something called trepanation, where the surgeon drilled into the skull. A crude tool drilling into your skull without anesthesia. Hard to imagine . . . just thinking about it hurts.

Modern surgical techniques made great strides in the eighteenth century by which time they had better instruments as well as a more advanced understanding of the internal organs and the nature and causes of various diseases. But still little in the way of pain relief. A painting by the Italian Gaspare Traversi shows an operation circa 1753. A man is bent over a table, held down by another, while the attending "doctor" pokes into an open wound with a sharp instrument. The man shrieks in pain. Behind, his wife prays.

These examples from the past are just the extremes. Imagine even every day pain, the kind that sends us whimpering to the medicine cabinet: toothaches, sprained ankles, headaches. There was nothing for them, not much anyway. Here, chew these leaves.

Today Americans spend $86 billion a year on back and neck pain relief alone. Tragically and counterintuitively in this age of universal pain control, the fear of pain has given birth to a movement to commit suicide rather than face it. Psychiatrists say it is the depression—suffering—in anticipation of pain that drives the suicidal impulse rather than the pain itself.

There is absolutely nothing wrong with pain relief. Our advanced ability to control pain is a modern miracle given to us by God through proper use of His creation and the application of man's ingenuity. Pain relief is one of our greatest gifts. But it is ironic that as we have come to control it so well, we have also become practically crippled by the very thought of it.

Some in modern life have a more positive attitude toward pain: athletes, for instance. They say, "No pain, no gain." Also, "Pain is just weakness leaving the body." These slogans are related to building up strength and endurance. At least they see pain as a unit of measurement, of getting stronger, faster, tougher, better able to throw blocks or take punches, better able to deliver pain to opponents. That said, the "no pain, no gain" mantra only makes sense of pain when it is directed towards an earthly end . . . what happens when that earthly end is no longer "in play"? What then?

Consider modern irreligious man for whom, other than building bigger muscles, pain is devoid of meaning. To him, pain must be among the greatest of all evils. In contrast, for believers, pain can be a punishment, a lesson, a test, or a tool, but at least there is a reason, something to take away, something to ponder or pray about. For modern man, it must be pure unmitigated evil and therefore a source of suffering and nothing else. If pain is something that makes no sense, has no meaning, then, well, what does make sense is that psychological suffering, spiritual suffering, or both will result.

We know from history and literature and more modern debates with atheists that it is the problem of pain, suffering, and evil that both keeps many people far from God and the Church and drives others away. It is a relentlessly powerful consideration: How could a loving God allow the pain and suffering we see every day? And perhaps what is most troubling to many: How could He allow such evil to strike the most innocent among us, the children?

British comedian and notorious atheist Stephen Fry is featured on a YouTube video answering the question as to what he would say to God if he ever met Him. Fry said, "I would say, 'bone cancer in children, what's that about? How dare you. How dare you create a world where there is such misery that is not our fault. It's not right. It's utterly, utterly evil. Why should I respect a capricious, mean-minded, stupid God who creates a world that is so full of injustice and pain?'"

The subjects of this book, the "Littlest Suffering Souls," had a different view, one that cannot be understood without an understanding of what the Church taught them about pain. Like many things Catholic, the Church's view of pain may seem strange viewed in isolation. It may be said that many aspects of the Faith can seem so to others and, truth be told, at times even to Catholics ourselves. We venerate the limbs of saints, after all. In the Diocese of Armagh, Northern Ireland you can venerate the head of St. Oliver Plunkett, kept there under glass for the faithful.

To many people in the world today, the Catholic teaching on pain may be just as strange, incomprehensible, and esoteric as that.

That said, not everyone in the world today runs from pain. Elite athletes embrace it. Cyclists in the Tour de France carry their bodies across 2500 miles of roads, including climbs of thousands of feet in the Alps and Pyrenees. They will ride hundred-mile stages each day for a solid month at speeds of thirty miles an hour or more. They say cyclists are in love with pain.

Football players play through pain. Sometimes they will have a cracked rib. If you've ever had one, you know how painful that can be. They play anyway. "Tape and go" is the mantra, though less so today than in the past.

Even the modern secular sweating it out in the gym every morning appreciates pain. They may not like it, like the marathoner, but they appreciate it. Maybe it is now a mock-able gym-cliché, to say nothing of a political slogan that had its fifteen minutes of fame, but in years past, you could hear them shout, "feel the burn" during aerobics class. The burn is pain, and they celebrate it. Pain means something is happening in their bodies to make them stronger. It may hurt, but they recognize the necessity of this pain in order to achieve their goal.

Modern secular workout warriors may appreciate this sought-out pain as a measure of physical advancement, but there it ends. How they view undesired pain from maladies and afflictions would be an entirely different thing, and that is that is the type of pain we consider in this book.

"Blessed be pain, sanctified be pain" is not something evangelicals would likely ever say. It comes from a little book called *The Way* by St. Josemaría Escrivá where he extols the importance of suffering in the life of the Christian. Escrivá says, "In our poor present life, let us drink to the last drop from the chalice of pain. . . . What does suffering matter if we suffer to console, to please God our Lord, with a spirit of reparation, united with him on the cross—in a word, if we suffer for Love?"

Let's talk first about reparation. This would be an utterly foreign concept to most other religions and even to our evangelical brothers and sisters. The central message of Our Lady of Fatima in that dusty field in Portugal one hundred years ago was that we must pray for the conversion of sinners and also make reparations for the offenses made against the Immaculate Heart of Mary.

The Immaculate Heart of Mary, which leads us to the Sacred Heart of Jesus, is offended continuously in this world through what people do and say and even think. But we can make up for this; we may make reparations for these offenses through offering our pain and suffering for that purpose.

Even more scandalous to some is that we can unite our suffering to His on the Cross. How is such a "uniting" possible if the Crucifixion was a discrete event in history with a beginning, a middle, and an end that happened a couple thousand years ago? The belief that no such uniting is possible is the very reason why most Protestants do not have the corpus on their crosses. It happened; He suffered then, and it is over. Catholics believe we can, in fact, unite our suffering to Christ's on the Cross and suffer with Him if our suffering is offered for that intention.

So right away we see enormous differences between Catholic belief and the belief of others, and it is only through this belief that the words and actions of the Littlest Suffering Souls can be understood.

Pope St. John Paul the Great published a magnificent Apostolic Letter on suffering in 1984 called *Salvifici Doloris* (salvific suffering). He teaches that "salvific suffering" is not just Christ's *but ours, too.* This may sound scandalous to many, but the saintly pope begins by quoting the Apostle Paul, "In my flesh I complete what is lacking in Christ's afflictions for the sake of his body, that is, the Church." He says the Apostle Paul celebrated his suffering when he came to understand its salvific meaning.

John Paul II tells us that Sacred Scripture is "a great book about suffering," and he lists a number of examples from its pages—danger of death, death of children, lack of offspring, homesickness, persecution, mockery and scorn—and he even lists specific body parts mentioned in Scripture: bones, kidneys, liver, viscera, and heart.

St. John Paul confirms what other monotheistic faiths believe: that suffering can be a punishment for sin and that suffering can be visited upon someone for the purposes of discipline and conversion. But the story does not end there; Catholic teaching on suffering soars to breathtaking heights. Man has his own share in the Redemption, the great and saintly pope tells us.

John Paul writes, "The witnesses of the New Covenant speak of the greatness of the Redemption, accomplished through the suffering of Christ. The Redeemer suffered in place of man for man. Every man has *his own share in the Redemption*. Each one is called to share in that suffering through which the Redemption was accomplished. He is called to share in that suffering through which all human suffering has also been redeemed. In bringing about the Redemption through suffering, Christ has also raised human suffering to the level of the Redemption. *Thus each man, in his suffering, can also become a sharer in the redemptive suffering of Christ.*"[3]

As you ponder that, consider that he goes even further. John Paul II agrees with the Apostle; we can do more than join in the sufferings of Christ, we can help accomplish the Redemption.

St. Paul writes to the Colossians, "In my flesh I complete what is lacking in Christ's afflictions" (Col 1:24). What could he mean by this? Is he suggesting that the Redemption of Christ is not complete? The pope helps our understanding: "It only means that the Redemption, accomplished through satisfactory love, remains always open to all love expressed in human suffering."

John Paul II says, "In this dimension—the dimension of love—the Redemption which has already been completely

---

3 Pope John Paul II, *Salvifici Doloris* (Vatican City: Libreria Editrice Vaticana, 1984), http://w2.vatican.va/content/john-paul-ii/en/apost_letters/1984/documents/hf_jp-ii_apl_11021984_salvifici-doloris.html.

accomplished is, in a certain sense, constantly being accomplished."⁴ Christ did not bring the Redemption to a close. The Redemption was not a one-off event. It continues today and tomorrow and the day after that.

Moving away from somewhat complex theology, let us consider the individual in everyday life. He may not understand the notion of sharing in the redemptive suffering of Christ that continues to this day. But he, at least if he is of a certain age and was raised Catholic, will be familiar with the term "offer it up," a concept foreign to our evangelical brothers and sisters.

Not long ago, I ran into a very fine evangelical woman of my acquaintance. She was suffering with breast cancer. I suggested that she offer up her pain for others. Give your pain to Christ for the sake of others. She was stunned. She had never heard that before, that our suffering can be offered up for the benefit of others. You could see her mind working on how wonderful that would be, how meaningful her pain could really become.

Every Catholic child from an earlier generation knew the phrase "offer it up." Don't like the spinach? Offer it up. Got a terrible cold? Who do you want to offer it up for? Let's offer it up for Aunt Mildred; she is sad today. This phrase can sadly become a meaningless cliché or even a weapon, but understood properly, its meaning is nothing short of staggering.

The Church teaches that our pain can benefit not only others on this Earth but also those who have died and are now in purgatory. That fact alone creates a chasm between

---

4 Ibid.

the Catholic understanding of suffering and that of evangelicals because they do not believe in purgatory.

But what is purgatory? The Church teaches that we cannot arrive in heaven until we are spotlessly clean of all sin
and the residue of sin. This is a tall order and requires suffering but suffering undertaken for that purpose. Pope John
Paul II banged his knee getting out of a car and he said,
"Thank you, Jesus." He was offering it up, purging his own
sins and helping others. He likely had a lengthy list of people who had died and were possibly in purgatory that he
was seeking to help. And we know he prayed for at least
two of the Littlest Suffering Souls by name.

We can even create sufferings or deprivations for the
purpose of training our bodies and souls for greater trials,
or to reduce our time, or that of others, in purgatory. These
are called mortifications, and when they are sought out,
they are something utterly foreign to other faiths. We eat
the hated spinach. We take the stairs. We leave something
on the plate, something that we love. We offer it up.

Consider prayer and suffering. The Church teaches that
among the most effective prayers are those carried out
without consolation. The contemplatives call this the Dark
Night of the Soul where God removes all consolation yet the
believer continues in his prayer for love of God alone. This
is not just for the ordained or consecrated. It is for us all. If
you read St. Teresa of Calcutta's letters published after her
death, you can see she suffered in this fashion for much of
her life, and that this is suffering of the highest but most
fruitful degree. This suffering brought about by dryness and
lack of consolation in prayer can perhaps most especially
be used to the great benefit of the sufferer as well as others.

The Littlest Suffering Souls "got" all this, perhaps on an intuitive level alone, but they understood that, for Catholics, pain can be the occasion of great blessings and spiritual fruit; it can be blessed and sanctified in such a way that it leads to the sufferer's sanctification.

Of course, what to do with suffering or how to respond to it does not address the more basic question posed by so many. Why does it exist in the first place? Why does anyone suffer? Why do children suffer? What about comedian-atheist Stephen Fry's legitimate question about bone cancer in children? Why that? Catholic bishop Robert Barron has an answer for Fry and other modern questioners.

Bishop Barron paraphrases God's answer to Job for a modern audience. "You can't possibly know because you are not me and you do not know everything."

Bishop Barron imagines one page of J. R. R. Tolkien's three-volume 1300-page *Lord of the Rings* being ripped out and "cast to the winds. It floats on the winds for months. It becomes further tattered, only bits of it remain here and there." Someone who has never read Tolkien "stumbles upon this fragment of a page, and reads one paragraph of this great sprawling novel." The paragraph he picks up is the scene of Frodo and Sam in Mordor "at the depths of their suffering." It's just one paragraph, and the man who picks it up thinks, "What a terrible story. Whoever wrote that must be some kind of monster to have written that." [5]

---

5 Bishop Robert Barron, "Stephen Fry, Job, and Suffering," *Word on Fire* video, 10:07, posted February 26, 2015, http://www.wordonfire.org/resources/video/stephen-fry-job-and-suffering/4671/.

The bishop explains, "That little paragraph belongs in a page, which belongs in a chapter, which belongs in a sprawling [1300] page novel. We who have read the whole book know that terrible suffering of Frodo and Sam is an ingredient ultimately in this comedy, ultimately in this great joyful and life-affirming story." The whole book cannot be judged or even remotely understood by that one paragraph. In the same way, Barron says, we live in a tiny fragment, one tiny sliver of space and time and that it would be the height of arrogance to suggest from this tiny glimpse that we can possibly know the whole story of God's creation. "The suffering of a child, bone cancer in a child is terrible, but is it nothing but terrible? Is it irredeemably terrible? Is it terrible, period? Or is it perhaps an ingredient in a much larger story? Is it possibly a route of access to a deeper and richer life?"[6]

And so we turn to the story of three children who "got it," children who embraced and lived the Catholic under-standing of suffering, and who, through their suffering and their approach to it, brought others to the Church and to Christ and perhaps to heaven itself.

---

6 Ibid.

6

BRENDAN OF GREAT FALLS

THE big black Suburban rolls up to the front of the Heights School in Potomac, Maryland, a suburb of Washington, DC and one of the toniest in the whole country. Joe Kelly jumps out of the front seat on his way to the boys' school run by the Catholic apostolate Opus Dei.

Joe trots away from the Suburban, but before he gets more than a few steps, the back window rolls down and out pops the head of a little boy who leans way out, spreads his arms, and shouts, really shouts, "Joe, Joe, what about me, Joe. Say good-bye to me, Joe. I love you Joe!" Not in the least embarrassed by this display, star-athlete Joe jogs back to give and receive a bear hug from his little brother Brendan. Joe turns away and Brendan shouts for good measure, "I love you, Joe."

Teacher Jeff Thompson tells this story today and even now, many years later, can't tell it without unashamed tears in his eyes. This was his very first glimpse of a boy who would change his life and that of many others. It is a story that, more than anything else, explains this boy Brendan. Utterly without guile, utterly without fear, bubbling over with love, this boy spread his arms and embraced this brother, the world, and all who came within his view, even those he never met.

Brendan's parents, Frank and Maura, were both born and raised in the Washington, DC area. Frank's father came from Spanish Harlem when it was still a bit Irish, and he grew up poor, according to Frank, "six children in one room." After a career in the Marines, rising to the rank of Lt. Colonel, Frank's father settled into a long career in the United States Senate, advising Democratic Senator Daniel Inouye of Hawaii. Frank's mother was a fourth generation Washingtonian raised in a socially connected family and also something of a beauty, once winning Miss Cherry Blossom—Washington, DC. Frank Kelly was born on the Marine base at Quantico, one of the key Marine training bases in the country.

Frank describes his family's faith as devout but also political. His father was always getting into tussles with the bishops: this, after all, was the time after Vatican II that led to great upheavals all over the Church. Frank's father went to daily Mass and said the Rosary every morning. Frank describes his mother as more retiring than his tough father, but she was also very faithful.

Maura comes from a deeply Catholic family. One of five children, she was raised in Arlington, Virginia by her corporate attorney father and her mother who volunteered at a pro-life pregnancy help center. Maura describes her mother and father as "super strong, very, very good Catholics." They were involved in the Cursillo movement—founded in Spain in 1944—that teaches laymen how to be leaders in the Faith.

Maura says her father was also involved in aspects of the charismatic movement. He spoke in tongues, for instance. Much of this sprang from a chance meeting her father had with the singer Pat Boone's wife on a plane, a meeting that changed his life. "He was never the same after that," says Maura.

Maura herself was once "slain in the spirit." And as a foreshadowing of things to come, the priest who laid hands on her said, "God has great plans for you." Maura, who has a wonderfully droll sense of humor, now says, "As life went on, I realized great plans doesn't necessarily mean super fun."

Though they had both attended Bishop O'Connell High School in Fairfax County, Virginia, they did not meet until they worked near each other in the George Bush White House in 1990. Maura was interning, and Frank, a holdover from the political affairs office in the Reagan White House, worked in the presidential correspondence office.

Congressman Henry Hyde's wife, who was also working in the White House, noticed Frank walking back and forth by Maura's office and told her, "He likes you."

On their second date, they decided to get married, which they proceeded to do in 1990.

Their daughter Mollie came along in early 1991, followed by Joseph in 1994. Brendan came three years later in 1997.

The Kellys live on what can only be described as a small farm in one of the most densely populated areas of the country, northern Fairfax County, Virginia, twenty-two miles northwest of Washington, DC in Great Falls, Virginia, also one of the most affluent areas in the country.

They live on nine acres that is home to horses, dogs, sheep, chickens, cats, kids, and friends, lots of friends. They bought the place for Brendan, and even the purchase of it was an act of Providence. They wanted a large property for Brendan, and this acreage came up for sale, but they found themselves bidding against wealthy contractors who wanted to break it up and build McMansions—the kind that dot the landscape of Great Falls.

The Kellys bid and bid and bid against the contractors and went to the very limit of their finances, finally "making a deal" with St. Joseph: If he gave them the property, they would never ever turn anyone away who came knocking on the door. You come to their house down a little rock road that veers off from a paved cul-de-sac, past multi-million dollar houses, and you come to a sign that says "Open Door Farm." And they meant it. They still do. "Open Door Farm," all are welcome.

When they moved to Open Door Farm, it was little more than a rundown barn and a small falling-down house. They did not build a McMansion. They built a ranch house, large certainly, but not gaudy, a manly house like you might see in Wyoming. Sitting with Frank and Maura in their enormous kitchen with huge windows open to the cool breeze and the sound of lambs bleating and the sight of horses trotting across green pastures, they tell their story, which is still as raw in the telling as it is in their hearts.

Maura says they didn't know Brendan had Down syndrome "until he was born." Maura was only thirty years old at the time, a low risk pregnancy. She declined any prenatal tests.

"And so he was born. It was the most beautiful birth in the whole world, no pain, easy peasy," she says.

"He just came out so peacefully," says Frank. "I'll never forget. He looked around quietly."

Though the doctors disagreed, Maura knew something was wrong. "Two days later, they confirmed he had Down's," says Frank.

Like many parents in similar situations, Frank and Maura were devastated. Maura says she had never even spoken to someone with Down syndrome, and "the doctors were terrible. He is not going to walk or talk," they said. The litany of limitations was overwhelming for Frank and Maura, "but he was so wonderful," she says.

It was remarkable to them because Brendan engaged visually from the start. As a tiny baby, he looked you in the eye. And he never cried, even when hungry or wet. He just laughed and smiled and looked you right in the eye. Maura says, from the beginning, Brendan's personality was "just love, love, love. . . ."

Brendan was born into a family with great faith. Frank is a supernumerary in Opus Dei, which means he was a daily communicant and committed to a rigorous daily set of "norms of piety." Maura, too, went to Mass every day. Frank and Maura tried to live continuously in the presence of God.

Frank Kelly is a big, jolly, generous man who has participated professionally in the highest levels of government and business. Besides working for two White House administrations, he has been a press spokesman at the Justice Department and has held a number of important posts in business. Today he is head of global government affairs for one of the largest financial services firms in the world.

Maura is a down-to-earth woman, utterly at home supervising the shearing of sheep and overseeing the regular, sometimes constant, flow of visitors who are welcome to just drop by. Maura is always ready with a cup of coffee or a glass of wine and an invitation to "stay a little longer, stay for dinner. . . ."

As overwhelmed as they initially were by Brendan's diagnosis—as wholly unprepared as they were—the Kellys were in many ways a perfect family to receive him. And so their Brendan had a head start in many ways, including in "taking on" the massive challenges he would face in his sadly short life.

Maura said it was a blessing that they did not know about Brendan in advance and that they were not sure there was a problem until a few days after his birth. "I was always happy that we never got the test done because he was right there in front of us, and it was like, okay, this is him. I'll accept him. This is who I love and who I have to change my vision for." The Kellys now receive phone calls from new parents of children with Down syndrome, and she tells them, "You have to mourn the child you think you were going to have."

Brendan's religious precocity showed itself even before he was two years old. Brendan loved to kiss the crucifix. "He loved Jesus," says Frank. They found him crying one day, which was unusual because he hardly ever cried, even when he was hurt. Brendan was crying and pointing to a statue of St. Joseph. Frank gave him the statue. Brendan kissed it and stopped crying.

But the Kellys had only a brief window of time to get to know their little guy before the shadow of death clouded their days because one day when he was two, Brendan got a fever that wouldn't go away. Not even antibiotics would help. Their doctor suggested a blood test. Oddly, Maura asked, "Will it show if he has leukemia?" Maura had a premonition that something awful was going to happen to Brendan.

The doctor called that night and he was weeping. "He has no platelets, no red blood cells at all. Get to the hospital right now." A bone marrow biopsy confirmed that Brendan had leukemia.

He was only two years old.

Brendan began a course of chemotherapy; the purpose of which is to kill all the blood cells because they carry cancer, and when the blood cells regenerate, the hope is they will be cancer-free. So they pumped the little boy full of chemo and steroids. The course of treatment lasted three years, one of intense treatment, and two of "maintenance." During that time, Brendan got sick almost all the time because his immune system was compromised, so he was in an out of the hospital constantly.

But along with the suffering would come countless graces.

It came about that one of the Kellys' neighbors who worked at the Department of State talked about Brendan at work. One of this man's colleagues, a Catholic, was going to Lourdes, and so he brought back a bottle of Lourdes water for Brendan. The neighbor, not even Catholic, said,

"I don't know how this works but here is a bottle of Lourdes water from one of my colleagues."

Not long after, Brendan was undergoing a very intensive chemo treatment, so intensive that almost as soon as the drug was pumped in, it had to be flushed out so that it would not damage his kidneys.

He was also being given a transfusion of an extremely potent anticancer drug that can cause renal failure. To prevent that, a "rescue" drug had to be administered at various times during the treatment. At the same time, he was being given huge amount of fluids intravenously to help support his kidneys. This was, of course, a highly complicated medical situation.

As it happened, a negligent nurse forgot to administer the rescue drug. Brendan was on the verge of renal failure that could have killed him.

Frank tells the story: "He had to pee. It was critical that he did. Otherwise it signaled he was going into renal failure. And, literally, we were standing there in the bathroom, and the little guy is standing there, tubes sticking out of him, and it's like, 'Come on, buddy, please pee,' because we think he's going to die."

Maura was crying. They could hear the nurses running down the hallway prepared to code Brendan and take him to the ICU.

Maura said to Frank, "Get the Lourdes water."

At the moment she touches his head with the Lourdes water, Brendan just explodes. Frank says, "He's peeing like a drunken sailor. He fills up the pee jug and the nurse comes in. We say, 'Is this good enough?' and the nurse says, 'Yes, that's good enough.' And Brendan was laughing and giggling because he was peeing so much."

Maura says, "We almost lost him a lot of times that first time."

Because of his compromised immune system, everything, even at home, had to remain sterile. Brendan's brother Joe and sister Mollie had a regimen where they would clean everything with Clorox wipes: every door handle, banister, and table. Visitors had to clean themselves with hand sanitizer before entering the house. This regimen lasted more than a year.

Brendan's cancer went into remission after a year of treatment and then he had to have two years of chemotherapy maintenance, with lots and lots of other drugs to help maintain him.

As mentioned above, along with the suffering came many graces, and it was during those two years that Brendan met Pope John Paul II, and a remarkable meeting it was.

The story begins with former senator and presidential candidate Rick Santorum and his wife, Karen, dear friends and neighbors of the Kellys. Rick Santorum was scheduled to be on an official US delegation to the Vatican to present Pope John Paul II with a congressional medal. Before they went to Rome, Karen Santorum went to the Kellys to get a picture of Brendan. They weren't home, so with the door usually unlocked, she went in anyway and got one. Before the ceremony began at the Vatican, she pressed Brendan's picture into the pope's hands and asked him to pray for the little boy in the picture. The pope kept Brendan's picture.

When Brendan was told that the pope was praying for him, Brendan cheerily said, "I am praying for him, too." From then on until the day he died, after praying for family, John Paul II led Brendan's nightly litany. Frank and Maura say Brendan developed a mystical bond with him.

Brendan's religious sensibilities sometimes took people by surprise. One day the Make a Wish Foundation came calling. This is the group that makes the wishes of sick kids come true. When they heard of Brendan's wish, they simply could not believe that the little boy really wanted to meet the pope. Certainly he wanted to play baseball with Cal Ripken or go to Disney World! They suspected Frank and Maura had put the idea into Brendan's head, so they shooed them out of the room. But it did no good. They questioned little Brendan alone for more than an hour. Brendan said over and over, "Me meet pope. Me meet pope."

And so the Make a Wish people called David Van Cleve, the Vatican desk officer at the State Department. As it turns out, Van Cleve already knew Brendan's name because he was in a prayer group with Robert Bork Jr., the son of the legendary Judge Robert Bork. A friend of Frank's, Bork Jr. had already introduced Brendan's name to the prayer group, so Van Cleve knew of Brendan and happily made the call to the Vatican. There are no coincidences in the often-charming world of God.

As a slight digression, as I relay Brendan's story, I am aware that I am doing what is commonly referred to as "name-dropping"; this is deliberate, but hopefully to be excused as it is done to emphasize a particular aspect of the lives of these "little suffering souls." Brendan and the others in this book were not peasant children tending their flocks. They were born into families of influence, families that inhabited a particular milieu: the power center of Washington, DC. In short, they, too, were born into a kind of spiritual desert, an environment in which the things of the world can so easily take precedence over the things of God, and they had—and still have—lessons to teach the inhabitants of that particular desert.

Brendan Kelly's much-desired visit with Pope John Paul II began in farce and ended in sublimity.

First, the farce. In Rome, waiting for the phone call that would give them the specifics of their visit—the when and where—the Kellys missed *every single message* left by the Vatican. The hotel simply did not give them the messages. When the hotel finally gave them the stack of messages, the meeting had already passed . . . that very morning.

Disaster.

In a stomach churning panic, the Kellys called the Vatican, and the nun with whom they spoke accused them of having "gone sightseeing."

"We didn't. We were right here in Rome. The hotel didn't give us your messages."

"Well, you missed the meeting. It was this morning. I am very sorry."

The Kellys begged and pleaded and prayed. The nun finally said, "Be at Castel Gandolfo tomorrow morning at 8 a.m." She also said she was going to call the manager of the hotel and let him have it.

Castel Gandolfo is the pope's summer-time residence seventeen miles south of Vatican City sitting on a hill overlooking magnificent Lake Albano. The Kellys got there early. The morning began with the pope's private Mass. The Kellys noticed they were the only laymen present as the room was full of seminarians, all Americans from the North American College, and one archbishop. A handful of nuns were standing in the back, and Frank got the feeling the Kellys had taken their place.

Such a Mass would have been sufficient for any faithful Catholic. To be in the presence of the Holy Father as he celebrates Mass is simply remarkable. But that was not all. After the liturgy, the group was ushered into a room where they waited for John Paul to greet them one by one. The Kellys, feeling very out of place, stood in the back. It should be noted that this was during Brendan's maintenance years of treatment, so they were also lugging around his bag of medication.

There was a stir in the room. The pope entered and took a seat on a large wooden chair, preparing to greet each person who typically will shake his hand or kiss his ring as a photo is snapped; maybe a few words are exchanged. All very quick, not hurried, but quick nonetheless.

Frank says, "Brendan got a look on his face like 'what are we doing way back here when the pope is way up there' and he took off running. I tried, but I couldn't stop him." The pope waved Frank back and welcomed Brendan at his side where they had a few words that no one else could hear. Frank says, "Whatever they said was intense. The Holy Father held Brendan's head in both his hands, and they were looking directly into each others eyes." And then Brendan stayed right there. He didn't move. He didn't even make a motion to move. He stood right there at the future saint's side the whole time. And they held hands.

Brendan is probably in every single picture taken that day. He was so tiny, a few feet high, standing there in his little suit holding the pope's hand. Between greeting other people, John Paul would turn and speak with Brendan, and this went on for the entire audience. Frank says the pope and Brendan laughed as they talked.

At the end, the pope left by the door through which he had come in, out into a long hallway. Everyone else was ushered out a door further back, but Brendan decided he wasn't finished with his new friend just yet. He could not get enough of John Paul II, and so he turned around and took off running, dodging the security team to get to the hallway. Standing at the entrance, he shouted, "Bye pope" and blew the pope a kiss. John Paul II paused, and then came back to Brendan. When he got close enough, Brendan extended his hand to shake the Holy Father's hand goodbye.

The pope bent slightly—it was the beginning of his decline—he took Brendan's little hand in his. Someone snapped what is now an iconic picture of Brendan Kelly reaching way up and Pope John Paul II reaching way down, their hands touching, their eyes meeting in mutual understanding, two Christian gentlemen bidding each other farewell. In the iconic photo, the pope's men, bishops, and aides, standing in the background against the far wall, can be seen beaming and chuckling, completely and utterly charmed. A sublime moment to be sure.

When the great holy man of the latter half of the twentieth century died, aides found a stack of photos in John Paul II's nightstand, photos of those for whom he had promised to pray. The Kellys are certain the photo of Brendan that Karen Santorum had swiped and pressed into the pope's hand was among them.

Brendan's way of the cross continued. All told, he had three bouts of leukemia; the first from three-and-a-half to six years of age, then again from ages ten to thirteen, and finally from fourteen to sixteen, the age at which he finally succumbed. The treatments were simply horrific each time, though the second and third were exponentially worse than the first. There were blood transfusions, chemotherapy, steroids, radiation, spinal taps, hundreds of pills every day, and eventually a bone marrow transplant. The steroids were particularly awful. They bloated him and made him feel twitchy and crazy. He hated those most especially.

His suffering notwithstanding, throughout his life, during sickness and health, Brendan had always displayed a deep religious sense belying both his age and his Down syndrome. Many who knew him believe he was a mystic. They believe he spoke to Jesus and that Jesus spoke back and that Brendan's guardian angel watched over him in a special way: more palpable, more tangible than the experiences most of us have with our own guardian angels.

Once, during his first bout with cancer, young Brendan wandered off from the family home in Great Falls. He thought he was following Frank to work. He simply disappeared, and his family could not find him. They looked everywhere, including in the woods nearby. Nine-year-old Mollie finally found him far away wandering down the street. Asked how she found him, Mollie said, "There was an angel in the driveway, so I followed him." Mollie was not given to such talk, and yet that is what she said and maintains to this day.

Yet another time, Frank was trying to get Brendan to nap. They were lying together in Brendan's bed with Brendan tucked up against Frank's massive frame. Like kids do, Brendan wouldn't settle down, and Frank was getting frustrated. Frank says that Brendan was looking off into the middle distance and talking. "I thought he was screwing around as all kids do when they don't want take a nap. I was about to bark at him to settle down, but something told me to stay calm and just ask him what he was doing. So I did: 'Buddy, who are you talking to?' I asked."

Brendan said, "Jesus" and pointed to a specific spot. There is nothing there, not even a crucifix. To this day, Father Alexander Drummond, pastor of the local church of St. Catherine of Siena, firmly believes Brendan was a mystic: that he saw and spoke to Jesus who was truly present to this little boy. Father recalls a time when Brendan was eight. He had been to confession. It was evening. Brendan spent a long time making his penance in one of the pews. When Brendan returned to his father, who was talking to Father Drummond at the back of the church, Frank said, "You must have been really bad to get such a long penance."

Brendan said, "I wasn't doing my penance. I was talking with Jesus."

"Yes, He's in the tabernacle."

"No, He's in the light above the tabernacle."

Father Drummond says, "The place was completely dark. There was no light above the tabernacle." When pressed about how authentic this might be, Drummond says, "I don't think he could make it up. He was not in any way deceptive. He did not have a desire to impress people or to mislead. There was nothing false about it."

It was Father Drummond who prepared Brendan for his first Communion and heard his first confession. "That is when he first came to my attention," says Drummond. Though Brendan had Down syndrome, Drummond says, "he knew enough to make his first confession and first Communion. He understood. He was very high functioning, and he was very excited." Drummond recalls "his absolute joy at wanting to receive Communion, to receive the Eucharist."

One of the more dramatic stories of his life occurred when Brendan was sick the second time. One of Frank's friends and business partners found himself in the midst of a terrorist attack, the one at the Taj Mahal Palace and Tower Hotel in Mumbai where the Islamic terrorists came ashore in rubber rafts, invaded the swank hotel, and went floor to floor methodically shooting everyone they saw, especially Americans.

The terrorists hit when Peter O'Malley was checking in. A six-foot-four-inch American, he correctly figured he would be an easy and early target, so he spent the next fourteen hours hiding out from room to roof, from bathroom to conference room to business center. People were being shot all around him. O'Malley was in touch with the bank's security who were watching the event on television and advising O'Malley where to go. At some point during the slaughter, O'Malley got in touch with Frank and asked for Brendan's prayers. He and Brendan had become phone friends during Brendan's second sickness. Some of

Brendan's treatments that second time took place in the middle of the night, and so Frank took to calling O'Malley in Hong Kong and putting Brendan on the phone and they would chat away. So O'Malley knew Brendan had powerful friends in heaven, and he asked for Brendan to talk to them. Later that night, Brendan went into Frank's office and told him, "Mr. O'Malley is going to be rescued tonight. Jesus told me." Roughly at that same time, O'Malley had made his escape from the building where 164 people were murdered.

Brendan's mom, Maura, says her son couldn't get away from God even if he wanted to. That was how close he was. She tells the following story. One day Maura called Frank home from the office. Brendan was sitting in his room deeply depressed. Maura had never called Frank to come home like that.

"What's the problem?" Frank asked.

"He's just so sad. I can't deal with it. I can't. He's just so sad."

Frank went home and found Brendan in his room where he had been for hours. "Why are you so sad, buddy?"

"He's not here."

"Who's not here?"

"Jesus. He's not here. He's gone. Where did he go? Where's Jesus?" Brendan didn't know that it was Good Friday. Frank assured Brendan that Jesus would return on Easter.

One of Brendan's talents was an uncanny ability to know when someone else was hurting. It was like a second sense. In those days, with Mollie and Joe as teenagers, the house was full of their friends. It was a great place to be, the large farm, large house, horses, fun Frank and Maura, and Brendan. Looking back on those days Maura says, "We had a lot of lost souls come through our house."

One of Mollie's friends came from a terribly broken home, and her confidence and self-esteem were non-existent. Her dad didn't want anything to do with her, and her mom was bipolar. The girl was depressed. Brendan spotted her pain and sidled up to her and became a real pain in the neck trying to cheer her up. This went on for a good long while. He would make stupid jokes and then launch into how God loved her. "Isn't God great? Don't you just love, God? Isn't He great?" Maura says that was Brendan's *modus operandi.*

The young girl once babysat for Brendan and they sat on the couch watching TV. Brendan kissed her cheek and snuggled with her. He told her how much God loved her and how much he did. She remembers it as one of the most memorable nights of her life. She found worth and love, love, love from young Brendan. He changed her life.

And he did this over and over with many others. The Kellys say this kind of "Brendan treatment" brought more than one of Mollie's friends into the Church. Maura says, "He was lobbying all the time."

Frank chimes in, "God's lobbyist."

Brendan's influence could touch the heart of a suffering girl as well as those in great positions of power. Perhaps the best exemplar of someone in the latter group would be a dear friend of Frank's, a well-known and even controversial public figure. A Catholic convert, he nonetheless has lived an irregular personal life. His situation was often talked about in the Kelly household. After all, they were close with him and wanted the best for him and his family.

This man loved Brendan dearly, and Brendan loved him. One day he was coming to Open Door Farm and Brendan's parents told Brendan, begged Brendan, ordered Brendan not to mention the gentleman's irregular situation. Brendan promised he wouldn't bring it up. There was a knock on the door. The gentleman walked in, was welcomed by Frank, and then Brendan ran in, gave him a huge hug, and immediately said, "I love you so much. God loves you so much. Jesus loves you, and I love you and," Brendan couldn't help himself, "Jesus wants you to do the right thing, because He loves you so much. All you have to do is the right thing."

The man broke down sobbing and had to leave. Brendan, God's lobbyist. When Brendan died, this man flew his entire family—his wife and eight children—in for the funeral.

The pictures from Brendan's life tell the tale about how well he was loved and how much he loved. They show a little boy, clearly but not profoundly Down's, at the center of things, the focus of joyous attention. One such picture shows him dancing at a wedding: white shirt untucked, arms spread wide, with a huge grin on his face, cousins and friends standing nearby laughing uproariously.

Another picture shows Brendan in the stands in the gym at the Heights School. Again, his arms are up and wide, and he wears a huge grin, obviously receiving some massive accolade. In fact, it was at his brother's graduation, and Brendan was being recognized from the podium even though he was not a student. Even so, he was a much beloved, perhaps the most beloved, member of the Heights community.

To this day, Jeff Thompson, one of Brendan's closest friends, gives a lecture in one of his classes at The Heights about Brendan. A huge picture of Brendan meeting the pope hangs in Thompson's classroom. Thompson's head shakes violently when he speaks. Early on Brendan asked him, "What's wrong with you?"

"I have Tourette's."

"That's okay. I have stuff, too."

Perhaps because of fear, lack of understanding, whatever, there tends to be a wall around the disabled, a wall that most people cannot breach, even if they feel guilty as they turn their gaze or walk away. Brendan broke down that wall for people. Actually, for Brendan, that wall simply did not exist. He willed it out of existence with his great joy and love.

What Thompson says is what you hear over and over and over about Brendan; he was full of love, utterly unashamed, utterly without guile, and the very center of attention. "Everyone wanted to be near him, everyone," said Thompson. He was the coolest kid at The Heights.

The Heights headmaster, Alvaro de Vicente, says Brendan had a "soul that every teenager wishes they had. There was something so innocent and pure and good and fun about Brendan that resonated with any teenager."

Brendan's Aunt Kelly McCabe, who lives nearby in Great Falls with her own large family, says Brendan was always the center of attention, though it was never a status he sought. She says it was just natural and something that he accepted with joy.

Brendan's deep faith in and love for God would have, if not for his afflictions, made him a natural candidate to be an altar boy. Happily, he had a pastor who could see past the challenges such a situation could present. It was when Brendan's leukemia was first in remission that Father Drummond asked him if he wanted to be an altar boy. Drummond had developed a huge altar boy program, boys only. At the 10:00 a.m. Sunday Mass, it remains quite common to see sixteen boys vested for mass.

When Father told him he would get to wear the black and white vestments of an altar boy, Brendan's eyes grew wide, "He got a faraway look in his eyes and said quietly, 'I love those.'"

Brendan was very high functioning for someone with Down syndrome, so much so that he wasn't above occasionally using it to get his way or get out of doing something. Maura often told others not to let him play the "dumb Down's kid." She told people to challenge him and that he was "crazy smart."

Once, the Kellys were having some major construction done on their house. One of the construction guys took to riding Brendan, really picking on him, in a kind of mean way. It was truly odd. One day when Brendan came home from school, the guy said in kind of a sneering and mocking voice, "Brendan, aren't you glad it's Friiiiiday. No more school tomorrow." Brendan gave him a deadpan look and said, "It's Wednesday, @#*%!." The rest of the crew collapsed in laughter. They guy stopped ribbing Brendan. They became friends, and when Brendan died, he cried like a baby at the funeral.

To show how quick-witted Brendan could be, consider this exchange. Asked by his psychiatrist—hired to help him through the rough times—what it was like to have cancer, Brendan said, "It's like driving in the car with Karen in the backseat." You have to know Will Ferrell's movie *Talladega Nights: The Legend of Ricky Bobby* to get the reference. Karen was the very live cougar that rode in the back seat of Ricky Bobby's race car.

Then there is the story about one of Brendan's doctors. As he was at the hospital quite frequently and given his infectious personality, Brendan was everyone's favorite. The doctors, nurses, and staff all loved him because he was so funny. They once hung a sign on his door that said, "Only Dancing Girls Allowed." One day a nun arrived to administer the Eucharist to Brendan. She saw the sign and danced across the room and gave him Communion.

His oncologist was a gruff and well-respected doctor named Marianna Horn. Even the nurses, who aren't afraid of anything, were a bit wary of Horn. So Brendan decided to call her Dr. Sweetie Pie, which he did for the rest of his life. She loved it.

After Brendan went into remission the first time, they did not see Dr. Sweetie Pie for five years. When the leukemia returned, Frank and Maura went to her office, and what did they see? Brendan's picture. That's the kind of impact Brendan had on people.

After that five-year lapse, Dr. Horn was devastated to hear the news that Brendan's cancer had returned. A cancer patient is considered cancer-free if they are in remission for five years. Pretty much every day for those five years, Frank and Maura checked Brendan's skin for those little red spots called petechia, pinpricks of blood that show the vessels are breaking. Sadly, that is exactly what they found on February 27, 2008.

The first time was hard. The second time was pure hell. If they had known the first time what the second time would be like, they would have considered the first course of treatment a walk in the park. The second time, Brendan spent almost every day and night in the hospital for two years. Whenever he was home, they had the ambulance service on speed dial because he would inevitably go septic, his blood pressure would crash, and he would nearly die.

Two brutal years of treatment ensued, and Brendan responded; that is, he did not die, but at what cost? His body was just brutalized. The course of chemo and steroids had left his body crippled. He had something called necrosis, bone death caused by chemo, in both hips and one knee. The pain was constant and intense and not treatable. He had to sit there and take it, and it made Brendan cry, this boy who never cried. It broke your heart to see him cry in pain.

A special surgery rejuvenated his bones to some extent. Told he would never walk again, he defied the odds and did so, but not well. He got stronger, sort of.

Brendan probably should have died that second time. That's what Maura says. She is convinced he stayed around to save her because she came to hate God. How could he have allowed this to happen to her boy? She could barely rouse herself to go to Mass. Father Drummond noticed that Maura often did not go to Communion. How could you when God is your enemy? During particularly tough treatments, Brendan would say, "This is for you, Mom." He knew what he was doing. He was offering his pain for his mother's return to God; he was bringing her back to the Faith.

Brendan was a real human being, not an angel, and like any other person, no matter how holy, he did not necessarily want that cup. He did not want to die. Father Drummond was present when Brendan told Frank and Maura that he didn't want to die, there was too much to do and too many places he wanted to see. Yes, Brendan suffered both in body and soul. But then, so too had the God he loved.

To help Brendan through the especially tough times, the Kellys got Brendan professional help: a psychiatrist who met with him frequently. She eventually stopped charging for the visits. She said, "Talking to Brendan is like talking to God." She later said his death was the most traumatic experience of her professional life.

Brendan once more went into remission, but it didn't last. Just as before, his family checked his skin every day, and within one year this time the dreaded petechia appeared. And so began the final act, the final months, one final, even desperate, attempt to save Brendan's life. It was time for a bone marrow transplant, the truest of Hail Mary passes.

The petechia appeared on May 4, 2011. And thus began an intense four-month wait for a proper donor to be found. There has to be a match, otherwise the body will reject the transplanted marrow. All the while, the cancer has to be kept in check through chemo but not too aggressively because Brendan's body would be so beat up by the eventual transplant that they could not weaken him too much beforehand. Maura said it was like walking a very fine line, "taking him to the threshold and not sending him over and killing him while you're waiting for the donor."

The Kellys went on a whirlwind tour of medical facilities around the country, visiting twelve in all, looking for the place with expertise in performing a bone marrow transplant on a boy with Down syndrome. Such a thing is rare even today. Down's people come with a whole unique set of medical problems that further complicate something like a bone marrow transplant. Some bluntly told the Kellys it wasn't worth it to try to save Brendan's life.

They chose Boston Children's Hospital because they had done eleven bone marrow transplants on Down's kids in twenty years. That's not a lot, but that was the most. They also chose Boston because it is still, to some extent, a Catholic town.

Finally, a donor was found in Germany.

The first step in a bone marrow transplant is full body radiation. You lie naked in a bunker-like room all by yourself and literally get your own bone marrow "bombed out." Your lungs are covered in metal so the radiation won't burn them out. You are connected to loved ones via speakers while they are watching a tiny screen with doctors in a NASA-like room nearby.

Brendan went through this for forty-five minutes to an hour twice a day for five days. The radiation sickness was horrible. Maura said Brendan was "sick, sick, sick." Brendan offered all of his suffering for others, for his Mom, for marital problems and personal problems of others they knew about, for men out of work.

Brendan played games during those long hours in radiation. They played a game of "Office" trivia. It was Brendan's favorite show; he was an expert, and it was him against Frank and Maura and all the doctors and nurses. Maura says, "It was everyone against Brendan and Brendan won. Every time. He crushed us all."

According to Frank, "It went like this: 'Season 3, Episode 4, Dwight said this about beets.' There was this little grainy image of Brendan lying only a few feet but a million miles away and his little squeak of a voice would say, 'They are the nectar of life.'"

And Brendan would be right and he would be laughing. They all laughed. By the end of the radiation treatment, there were five or six doctors and four or five nurses gathered around the tiny screen playing the game with Brendan. He beat them all over and over again.

It was during this time that he may have saved the life of little Bella Santorum. The daughter of Rick and Karen Santorum, Bella had been born with among the rarest of Down's afflictions, Trisomy 18. Diagnosed in utero, the Santorums were advised to abort her. They said she would live only a few hours after birth. In fact, she survived, but, as Santorum will tell you, even a cold could kill her. "A simple cold and it's all hands on deck," he says.

Brendan prayed for Bella all his life. During those long days of total radiation, you could hear him offering his suffering up for Bella. "Bella, I love you," he would say over and over. The Santorums believe Brendan saved her and has kept her alive since.

His own bone marrow now utterly gone, the doctors dripped the donor marrow into his bones and waited. His body reacted well. It seemed to accept the marrow, and his red blood cells—a whole new blood type—began to

grow enough so that it was decided he could go home after
a while.

His immune system, though, was now completely compromised. Only one visitor other than family was allowed
inside Open Door Farm. That Christmas, they set Brendan
up outside on the front porch with a heater, bundled up in
electric blankets, and he would receive visitors who were
not allowed to touch him.

Father Drummond talks about how visitors were often
a massive test for Brendan. The near constant visitors who
wanted to see him wore him down mentally and physically.
Yet he never turned anyone away. Father Drummond tells
the story about a time when a particular woman was on her
way: Brendan said he wished she wasn't coming, but when
she arrived, "you could not tell that he wasn't completely
thrilled to see her."

In those final days, the family actually took him to one
of Joe's basketball games at The Heights gym. There was
Brendan, wrapped all in blankets, head as big as a balloon,
surgical mask over his face so he wouldn't catch anything
and die. They sat near a door that they kept open to keep the
air circulating. It was winter and cold outside. The referee
demanded they close the door. Jeff Thompson sidled up to
the Ref, pointed to Brendan, and explained. The door stayed
open. Alvaro de Vicente says, "Whatever team he was hang-
ing out with would become a Brendan-centered team."

What Brendan went through for the rest of his short life
is nothing short of biblical, the tests of Job and Jesus in the
Garden. Though he lasted another year and a half, though
he returned to school in fits and starts, it was a time of
great pain.

At one point they had to go into the hospital two or three times a week for eight to ten hours a day for a treatment to kill the blood's t-cells. "Mom, this is for you today," he would say, still trying to get her back to loving God.

At St. Catherine of Siena Church in Great Falls, parishioners were praying for Brendan. All over the world they were praying for Brendan. One frequent sight at Sunday Mass was of Father Drummond walking down the center aisle of the nave, into the narthex, out the front door to the curb where the big black Suburban would be waiting. A window would slide down, and Drummond would lean in and offer the Eucharist to a swaddled up and dying Brendan. Frank called it "drive-through Jesus." Everyone at Mass knew, and through their shared pain, they loved it. They loved Brendan.

No matter what pain or suffering he experienced, Brendan's love of Christ never wavered. Maura says Brendan "just couldn't get away from God. He was so immersed in God that even when he wanted to, he couldn't get away. Even if he wanted to watch a stupid show, he couldn't get away" because God always intruded upon his consciousness.

Kelly says Brendan prayed constantly for others and that his special concern "was suffering children, marital problems, and men who didn't have jobs or needed help with them."

At one point he came down with graft versus host disease, which caused huge ugly sores all over his body that told them that his body was rejecting the foreign bone marrow. Frank says, "They oozed. They were disgusting. And painful." Though Brendan hung on for a while longer, this was the signal that the end was near.

In those final days, Brendan had to have someone sleep with him every night to be there in case he needed help. He weighed two hundred pounds and was bloated because of the drugs. Moreover, he had those graft versus host sores all over his body. Most nights, it was Maura who slept with him. Kelly pestered her sister to let her do it, to let her sleep with Brendan, to give Maura a break.

Only one time did heroic Maura take her sister up on it. Kelly recalls helping Brendan into bed that night. Because of the sores, about the only place she could touch him was his head. "I was helping him into bed and he says to me, 'Aunt Kelly, I am so happy. I love Jesus so much.'"

Aunt Kelly didn't sleep a wink that night. She says she couldn't. She says she didn't even want to. "I couldn't sleep the whole night. I felt like I was sleeping with Jesus. I could just feel it. I didn't want to miss a minute of it. I just wanted to treasure this." She says sleeping with Brendan that one night was "like a gift." Maura said to her, "How do you think I feel every single night?"

The pain of those days still weighs heavily on Frank and Maura, both of whom begin to weep in their kitchen as they discuss Brendan's final pain and suffering.

They remember those final days in the hospital. He was on a ventilator. "His lungs were filled with fluid." Even the ventilator was doing damage to his lungs. Had he lived, perhaps six months or a year, he would have had to live in rehab for the rest of his life.

They fought for him as long as they could. He fought hard for his whole life. But in the end, his body was just too beat up. They couldn't put him through it any longer. They decided to let him go, to take him off the ventilator. Before they did, though, Maura had one last idea. Brendan always wanted to be confirmed. And so he was, right in his hospital bed. Father Drummond had to call around for the oils they needed, as it is normally a bishop who confirms. There is a picture of this: Mollie and Joseph—his siblings and now his confirmation sponsors—standing above Brendan and holding his shoulder, an utterly stricken look on their faces, and Father Drummond reaching out and touching oil to Brendan's forehead. You have to think that room was full of angels and that Jesus and Mary were present and that Brendan knew they were there.

Hours later, Brendan passed away.

The night before the funeral, the family greeted well-wishers at Brendan's church. The line stretched down the center aisle and out the front door and lasted for hours. It was estimated more than two thousand people showed up for the wake, coming in from all over the country and from all over the world. Frank, Maura, Mollie, and Joe stood at the foot of the altar and shook every hand and hugged every shoulder. The turnout showed that Brendan's reach in this life was broad and deep and vast. President George Bush wrote a private letter of condolence to Frank and Maura. Not bad for a life many today would say was not worth living.

The church was packed again for the funeral. It was estimated that more than two thousand people showed up. The choir from The Heights sang. Grown men and teenage boys, masters of the universe and construction workers wept openly and unashamedly. Father Drummond gave the

homily, "He is an extraordinary boy and not because he had
Down syndrome or leukemia but because of his immense
and intense faith. Brendan's best friend is Jesus. To Brendan Jesus was just as tangible and present as you and I."

Drummond quoted Father Benedict Groeschel who once
said about Brendan, "He is a suffering soul through whom
many will be brought to salvation."

After the final blessing, Father Drummond invited a
singer from the Old Brogue, a central meeting place in
Great Falls Village that Brendan loved, to play Brendan's
favorite song, Vince Gill's "*Go Rest High on That Moun-
tain,*" the refrain of which is as follows:

> Go rest high on that mountain
> Son, your work on earth is done.
> Go to heaven a-shoutin'
> Love for the Father and the Son.[7]

They buried Brendan in a private plot in the old family
parish near the generations-old family lake house in upstate
Pennsylvania where he loved to swim and ride around in
the family boat for hours on end with his numerous cousins, aunts and uncles, and grandparents. They buried him in
the vestments of an altar boy, but not the black and white
ones he loved so much. Those are for boys who have not
yet been confirmed. But Brendan had been confirmed, even
if just hours before he died. So Brendan wore the maroon
and white cassock that confirmed boys get to wear. He
would have loved them.

---

7 Written by Vincent Grant Gill • Copyright © Kobalt Music Publish-
ing Ltd.

MARGARET OF MCLEAN

FOR years, a picture of Margaret Leo has stood on the desk of Justice Clarence Thomas at the United States Supreme Court. It is framed in Popsicle sticks that Margaret fashioned herself.

Influential think tank president Edward Whelan credits Margaret Leo with interceding to save his father from a debilitating disease and certain death.

Patrick Fagan, former Bush administration official and head of a think tank on marriage at Catholic University of America, keeps Margaret's prayer card nearby and uses it often.

While it's true that Margaret's father is a friend of these men, they do not revere Margaret because of him. They revere her and even ask for her prayers because, as Whelan's father said about Margaret one day on a Northern Virginia baseball field, "I just met a living saint."

Leonard Leo is among the most influential men in Washington, DC. He is executive vice president of the Federalist Society, an organization of law students and lawyers that includes federal judges and Supreme Court justices. Leo is a close adviser to US senators and even to presidents. He was especially close to President George W. Bush, at one time running Catholic outreach for the Bush White House. Along with former Reagan chief of staff Ed Meese,

67

former White House counsel C. Boyden Gray, and lawyer Jay Sekulow, Leo was among the group called the Four Horsemen who advised President Bush on nominations to the Supreme Court. President Bush once met Margaret and referenced her in a speech he gave later that day.

Leonard witnessed death early in life. His father passed when he was a toddler, and he was raised in the home of his grandparents and was later adopted when his mother remarried. While his parents and grandparents practiced the Faith, it was not as intense a practice as what came later in Leonard's own home.

Leonard met his future wife, Sally, when they attended middle school in New Jersey. Sally was raised in a Presbyterian home where their faith was practiced, at least on an every-Sunday basis. Sally credits her grandmother with instilling in her a love of prayer.

She laughs that as a Protestant in college, she nonetheless went to Catholic Mass "five times every weekend." That's because she played the organ. Sally joined the Catholic Church the year she and Leonard graduated in 1987. They married shortly thereafter in 1989. Like any young couple, they had no idea what lay in store for them even a few years hence.

They say they were not fervent Catholics in those early years, attending Sunday Mass but not much more. Sally said she went to confession no more than once every year. Leonard says they were "observant Catholics in all respects . . . but with none of the bells and whistles" that came later under the tutelage of Margaret.

Audrey with her parents, brothers, and sisters at home in Paris in September 1989.

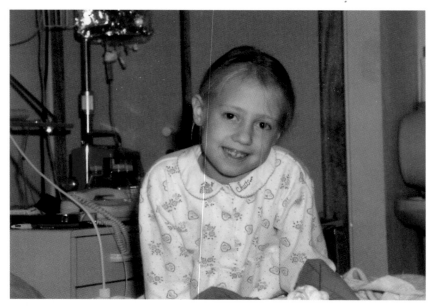

Audrey on her hospital bed, two months after the diagnosis.

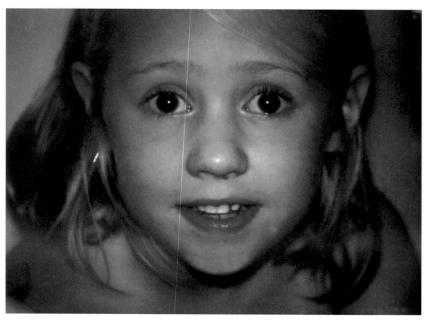

A close-up of Audrey at age four.

Summer 1989: Audrey playing in her grandparent's garden in France. Always fun-loving and ready to entertain!

Audrey soon after her bone marrow transplant, in the sterile "bubble".
Her sense of fun could not be defeated! (*opposite*) After the private
Mass with the Holy Father, Pope St. John Paul II in May 1991. Audrey
had only a few weeks to live.

Brendan (4) shakes the hand of Pope St. John Paul II during his "Make-A-Wish" trip in September 2001.

An infectious smile!

Brendan (9) with siblings Mollie (15) and Joe (12) in 2006.

Brendan and a feline friend.

Margaret's Confirmation Day, November 2007.

With Bishop Paul Loverde of the Diocese of Arlington and confirmation sponsor Katie Hickman Wood.

With Supreme Court Justice Clarence Thomas.

(*left*) Playing in the snow with siblings Anthony and Elizabeth. (*right*) Margaret loved holding babies. Shown here with baby brother Thaddeus.

A beautiful smile!

Margaret loved to organize family photos.

Margaret was conceived toward the end of 1991, and within fourteen weeks, they suspected something was wrong. Sally says, "I got a call at my office from my doctor telling me my AFP levels[8] were abnormal. And he wanted me to come in for further testing. And my next question was, what do I do about it anyway? And his answer was that many people decide to abort. That was out of the question."

Sally even declined an amniocentesis, which could have further harmed her unborn child. Still not sure of Margaret's medical condition, they went into a series of sonograms that increasingly showed a splaying of their baby's spine and what's called a "lemon sign" of the head. All of this was profoundly bad news for their unborn child. All the signs pointed toward a diagnosis of "myelomeningocele," or the most severe form of spina bifida, essentially a death sentence for most in this day and age. Children so diagnosed these days have virtually no chance of being born. Rather, most are aborted. Doctors, parents, and society in general are in lockstep about that. The argument is that such children are a burden too great to bear. They are expensive burdens on our healthcare system. They are a burden on the family. They say the child's quality of life would be so diminished as to be not worth living. It is a shock to many doctors, and very likely a scandal, that some parents—like the Leos—choose to bring such an unworthy child to term. Fortunately for Sally and Leonard, their doctors were supportive of their choice of life for Margaret. Because Sally declined an amniocentesis, the diagnosis would not be

---

8 Alpha-fetoprotein tests are a screen for possible abnormalities in unborn children.

verified until Margaret's birth, but preparations were made, including discussions with a neurosurgeon.

Even though she was determined to carry the child to term, Sally was, nonetheless, fixed with great anxiety. They hired a neurosurgeon to be prepared for the child's birth, and they decided on a C-section so her body would not be further traumatized by a vaginal birth.

Today Sally says, "The whole concept of having a child that wouldn't have the kind of childhood I had was sad, really, really, sad." She did not want the child to be born: She wanted her to remain safe in her womb for as long as possible. Sally says she was "scared the night before because I felt she was safe in utero. And I was scared as to what would happen. I wanted to keep her safe."

Margaret Leo was born by Caesarean section on August 26, 1992.

The doctors swept her immediately into the natal ICU, but before they took her away, Sally saw her eyes.

"I have a searing memory of seeing her eyes across the room. I was lying down on the table, and they were finishing the C-section. And she was in the little bassinet. And they were wheeling her out of the room, and I saw her eyes. They were beautiful. It was beautiful that her eyes were open, and I got to see her because I didn't get to hold her. That was it."

Margaret had an open neural tube defect, which means from a certain point down, her spine is not fully formed. In such a case, a sack develops: a sack that is a mass of nerves and fluid that has to be perfectly placed into the back and then the back closed. Risk of infection is high, and the surgeon must work very hard in placing the sack back properly. The severity of Margaret's situation was compounded by the fact there was not enough skin to close her back.

Before this remarkably complicated surgery, they baptized Margaret. If she died, she would have the mark of Christ on her soul. Her family made sure of that.

The surgery was long, very long, agonizingly long—all afternoon and into evening. They had to call in a plastic surgeon to close her back because of the lack of skin. All told, the operation took eight hours.

Margaret had a veritable litany of medical crises. In recovery, she developed hydrocephalus, which is a buildup of spinal fluid in the ventricles of the head. She had virtually no cerebellum, the part of the brain that is key to motor control. She was apneic, meaning she would occasionally stop breathing. She had Chiari II malformation where her brain develops in a place lower than it should, down into her neck, which can cause problems with breathing and swallowing as well as severe reflux, which can lead to regular vomiting—something Margaret did often for the rest of her life. She had syringomyleia, which is a cyst of fluid in the spinal cord that can cause a loss of sensation in the hands and feet and eventually paralysis. Margaret had no feeling below her chest. Her marked speech disability was likely due to some combination of these defects.

Margaret was lucky in two respects. Not long ago, children with spina bifida would die of infection because doctors did not know how to close up the back. And they would also die because there was no such thing as a shunt, something that came to loom large in Margaret's life.

A ventricular-peritoneal shunt is a tiny device placed in the skull that drains spinal fluid that builds up in the brain down through a tube placed under the skin to the abdomen where the fluid then drains into the peritoneal cavity and is absorbed by the body.

The shunt saved her in those early days, kept her alive through her short life, caused many medical emergencies, and may have killed her in the end. All told, Margaret had to have three shunts in the course of her life and experienced many "close calls" in which she would experience severe headaches for several hours due to a partial or temporary failure of her shunt.

Her medical problems persisted her whole life. She was in and out of hospitals for any number of things. For her bent spine, she had to wear a brace that covered her entire torso. Ultimately the doctors determined she would need scoliosis surgery, and two titanium rods were placed in her back. Leonard said the surgery "went really bad."

Afterward, she got an infection from a moderately resistant strain of bacteria called Enterobacter. They had to open her back and clean it out. Leonard says that was the time she was nearest to death. Her blood pressure "was at rock bottom." She landed in the hospital for two weeks on an IV drip of antibiotics. According to her father, "She was totally washed out. I'd never seen her like this before. It was sad." She was on antibiotics for a year, a central line feeding her a drug called Cipro at home for six weeks followed by oral antibiotics that had to be crushed and mixed with yogurt. Ultimately, the surgery failed to straighten the lower half of her back.

Margaret was confined to a wheelchair her entire life. Because of her curved spine, you always saw her leaning to one side, but you also always saw her smiling. You always saw her happy.

The Leos insist that Margaret never suffered severe prolonged pain and early on, suggested she might not have a place in this book alongside Brendan and Audrey, who suffered great pain through long stretches of their lives.

There is a distinction between pain and suffering. One may suffer without experiencing any bodily pain, certainly. Christ suffered in the Garden. The Leos suggest that Margaret was not in prolonged, great pain; after all, she was paralyzed from the chest down. Neither did she suffer emotionally in that she never expressed sorrow and sadness for her condition. She could never run with other kids, never play their games. She did not have any close friends her own age, and someone with such a severe disability sometimes seems to have a wall around them anyway, a wall that, as noted earlier, most people are afraid to breach.

But without a doubt Margaret suffered great evil, which is a deprivation of the good. She could not stand, walk, or run because her legs did not work that way or in any way at all. She could not eat anything other than the blandest foods because her system could not take anything else. She vomited all the time. She had intellectual disabilities, not like Down syndrome, but disabilities that made learning difficult and slow. She was in and out of hospitals her entire life. In these ways and many others, Margaret Leo experienced great evil.

But she experienced it, underwent it, bore it even with great beauty. When Margaret vomited, even in public, she never complained. She dutifully allowed her mother to clean her up. She then simply went back to whatever it was she was doing.

Those titanium rods doctors inserted in her back to keep her spine from bending even more? Those rods bent instead. Her spine bent those titanium rods. She was the little crippled girl who bent titanium rods. One of them ended up protruding through the skin of her neck, and even then, she did not complain. Leonard keeps the rods in his office at the Federalist Society to remind him what a really bad day would be like.

Though she could not walk or run or play with other kids, she never complained. Her brother Anthony says she would get frustrated sometimes that she could not do certain things. Even so, that was a rare occurrence, and, in fact, she enjoyed watching other children do all the things she couldn't. Sally says, "Margaret took great joy in watching other kids."

Margaret's father, Leonard, says she had a "simple yet profound connection to God—not mystical—she knew Jesus was God without any sense of the doctrine." That is how her faith can be summed up. It was profound yet simple. The truest things are also the simplest. She knew Jesus was God, not in the way we sometimes know it—sadly, all too often superficially—but profoundly, interiorly, intensely. Jesus was an utter yet simple reality to her, like the color green, or fresh air, or the man honking back there behind the family van. Utterly real.

When Margaret was little, she came to love religious things: books, statues, and other holy objects. Even before she could read, she would page through religious books over and over again. She had a great love for priests.

When she was four or five, she spotted Bishop John Keating heading down the center aisle of the cathedral after greeting parishioners on Easter Sunday. She called after him, "Pope! Pope!" chasing him in her little wheelchair.

When she was a little older and Sally took her to daily Mass, Margaret asked to go back to the sacristy to say hello to the priest she knew. This became a regular thing, so regular that she insisted upon going back even if they didn't know the priest. The Leos got to meet and know a lot of priests because of this little apostolate of Margaret's.

The Leos say she loved priests because they brought Jesus in the Eucharist. Margaret was absolutely devoted to the Eucharist. You could see her there with Sally almost every day sitting in the north transept at the Cathedral of St. Thomas More in Arlington, a daily sight of devotion: Sally's devotion to Margaret, and Margaret's to the Holy Eucharist. Margaret's thanksgiving after receiving was intense, and she could be heard saying, "Thank you Jesus for coming to me in Communion today." No lengthy thanksgiving from St. Thomas Aquinas for Margaret, rather something simple, one that would have moved the Dumb Ox himself, something so simple and profound especially coming from the little girl twisted to one side in her wheelchair. "Thank you, Jesus, for coming to me in Communion today," she would say out loud every time she received the Sacrament. Other parishioners heard this simple thanksgiving. They heard it every day. Years later, a woman approached Sally at church and reminded her that Margaret would say that out loud and how moved she was at the time and how even now she uses the same simple prayer of thanksgiving.

Margaret's special vocation was kindness to strangers. She loved to talk to strangers, everywhere. She knew the cashiers at the grocery story. She knew their names. She knew their birthdays. That was one of her opening gambits. "What's your name? When's your birthday?" You'd hear that in the elevator. Looking down, you'd see her gentle smile, and you'd have to answer. She also wanted to give and receive hugs, especially to and from priests. She loved that, insisted upon that.

She was naturally and intensely innocent and modest, and she saw only innocence in others. In the elevator one day, she saw a woman in a revealing top, and she wondered if the woman was going to the pool. No one would dress like that in Margaret's world unless she was going to the pool.

Kathryn Hickman Wood, a close family friend who often babysat, said Margaret would call her weekly and ask, "Are you happy?" And they would talk about saints and feast days. Wood says night prayers for Margaret would go on and on because she would pray for people by name: family, friends, strangers, priests. She never left anyone out, and her list was always growing. Wood credits her choice to become a special education teacher to her time with Margaret.

Father Ed Hathaway, a parish priest of the Diocese of Arlington, Virginia, says she was intense in her faith, direct and "tenacious." She would insist, "We have to go to Mass." In addition to priests, Hathaway says she especially loved angels.

Margaret's tenacity when it came to the Faith is shown by her single-minded determination to be confirmed and her thoroughgoing excitement at that prospect. Leonard says it was a countdown of more than two years. He laughs as he recalls, "It's just like every day, 482 days left until I get confirmed. It's impossible to have your daughter so excited about the Holy Spirit and a sacrament like that and your mind not be opened to something bigger."

Leonard says she told everyone about it. At one time, she believed that a dove would literally alight on her. In her almost unreadable scrawl, she carefully, slowly, and meticulously wrote out all of the gifts of the Holy Spirit, along with their definitions. The whole process had an effect of deepening the devotional life of her parents, Leonard and Sally.

Margaret may have never known the temptation to do evil, though real evil was sometimes present to her in a very real way, and she was highly sensitive to it. When she was four, a demon haunted her in dreams. Sally says, "She was so clear about it, and it had a name." One day at the Church of St. Philip in Arlington, Margaret noticed a statue of Our Lady of Guadalupe. "She immediately went to the statue and pointed to the black moon that's under Our Lady's feet and she said, 'That's him.'" Indeed, the upturned black moon—the Luna Negra—under Mary's feet, in what is the only artistic image created entirely by God and not by man, appears to be a set of horns. It appears Our Lady is crushing evil incarnate.

Her sensitivity to evil was such that one evening the family was watching *Sleeping Beauty* on television, and there was a scene where the evil queen turns into a dragon.

Margaret took one look and wheeled herself out of the room. Leonard says she wasn't afraid; she didn't cry, but she insisted that the dragon was what came to her in dreams and she did not want to have anything to do with such evil things. She refused even to be in the presence of evil.

Margaret hardly ever cried, was hardly ever frightened. In fact, the only time she was ever frightened or might cry was when Sally was not within earshot. She was so dependent on Sally for everything. If she was alone and unsure, she would call out, "I love you." If there was no answer, she would call out again, and again, until Sally answered, "I love you, too."

Margaret could be a nag, however, but only about things of the Faith. She insisted upon daily Mass. "When are we going to Mass?" "We have to go to Mass." Before Leonard was a daily communicant, she would ask him at the end of the day, "Did you go to Mass today?" To get Margaret off his back, Leonard became a daily communicant.

Under Margaret's urging and tutelage, the family's faith deepened.

Perhaps her closest friend on this earth was her younger brother Anthony, who was her nearly constant companion, especially when they lived in an apartment in Arlington and even after they moved to a house in the suburb of McLean, Virginia. Now a strapping six-footer, in those days, he was a skinny waif.

Living with her had to have been difficult, but no one says so. Anthony did everything with her in mind. Whatever he and his other siblings were doing, they brought her into the action. It was just the way it was. He recalls the times they wanted to spy on their parents talking in the living room, and they had to sneak down the hall to do so. As a matter of course, they could not forget Margaret, so they would slide her off the bed and onto a mattress that they would pull down the hallway.

Because she was so confined and was homeschooled and they lived in an apartment for most of those years, she never developed any friends of her own. Anthony says she did not seem to mind. She did not complain and was joyful when Anthony would bring his friends around. "The simplest things would make her happy, like my friends coming in to say hello," he says. "I know now she was more than satisfied with those interactions. She was very happy giving everyone a hug and then back to coloring."

He repeats what everyone says about her, "She liked simple things. Coloring. Mac and cheese. Doing stickers." He says she saw beauty in these simple things, that she saw beauty in things that were not objectively beautiful. And he says her faith could not have been simpler or more profound. "I love Jesus because he died for me" was the extent of it.

He says she had a passion for feast days. He laughs remembering her insistence on celebrating the Feast of Kateri Tekakwitha. "We didn't know who she was, but we were going to celebrate." According to Anthony, his sister's reverence for priests sprang from her understanding that they had "amazing responsibilities. She truly knew the sacredness of the Eucharist, which is why she revered the priest." During Mass, like most kids, Anthony would be playing with his shoes, playing with the kneeler, not paying attention. He says, "She struggled with regular things, but when it came time to pray, she would pray." He still remembers her thanksgiving and the daily visits to the priest in the sacristy. Even then he knew these were special things even if he did not share her enthusiasm.

Anthony remembers the day she died as if it were yesterday. He says before they moved to the McLean house, they shared a room. When they moved, however, they got their own rooms. Because he was so used to sleeping in the same room with her, his habit was to leave his room and sleep "curled up at the foot of her bed. I don't know. It just gave me comfort."

However, on that day—July 5, 2007—he was in Leonard and Sally's room, and he remembers a great deal of commotion. Leonard came in and told him "not to wake up, stay in bed." But Anthony felt a sense of urgency. "To this day, I don't know why. I got up and the ambulance was pulling away. I never once thought about death before that day," even though she had been rushed to the emergency room before. Anthony stayed in that room for two hours praying that his sister wouldn't die, "but somehow I knew she was going to die that day. I kept calling, but they wouldn't pick up, so I knew."

Margaret had a severe medical crisis that July 5, 2007 morning. Leonard carried her from her bed and laid her on the floor near the front door and called the ambulance. Sally went about getting all the things she would need for spending the next several hours in the emergency room. They had been through this before. Laying there, Margaret said, "Are you coming? I'm okay." But she wasn't.

The Leos took a moment to call Leonard's mother. "We are taking her to the emergency room and it's serious."

"No, it's going to be okay because I had a dream and Margaret told me it's going to be okay."

The Leos believe that was Margaret telling Leonard's mother she was really okay, that she may have been gone, but she was all right and not to worry. Margaret's heart likely stopped before the sirens began to blare, which was a blessing because she hated loud noise.

There were no spiritual fireworks in Margaret Leo's life, none that you could see or hear anyway. She led a profoundly sheltered life that was highly restricted. She met and became friends with very few people outside her immediate family. And her faith was as simple as simple can be.

But there is more to her story, as evidenced by what followed her death.

Not long after her death, the Leos were invited to spend some time on the California ranch of family friend Rob Arkley, a family get-away to begin healing. Before arriving at the ranch, they spent the night in a hotel in San Francisco. Because Leonard is a frequent traveler, the hotel provided a big dish of candy in the room. Margaret's sister, Elizabeth, who was six at the time, rushed and placed her hands in the dish and found a Sacred Heart Medal at the bottom. Odd that something like that would appear in a hotel candy dish, especially one in rabidly secular San Francisco. Granted, one Sacred Heart Medal does not make a miracle.

However, on their final day at the ranch, as they were preparing to leave, Sally was cleaning the floor, and she swept up a Sacred Heart Medal. It was not the one they found in the dish in San Francisco. It was another one! Their host, Rob Arkley, was not Catholic at the time and says he did not leave it there. The house was a little-used guest residence. Leonard got in touch with the previous guest, radio talk show star Laura Ingraham, and asked her if she had left a Sacred Heart Medal in the house. No, she hadn't.

Do two Sacred Heart Medals equal a miracle? How about a third?

Not long after the ranch vacation, another Sacred Heart Medal appeared. A woman coming to meet Leonard says she found a Sacred Heart Medal in her airplane seat. Just that morning, Leonard had been complaining about how much he missed Margaret.

Margaret is named for St. Margaret Mary, who was given the Sacred Heart devotion. Margaret, too, had a life-long devotion to the Sacred Heart of Jesus. The Leos are convinced the appearances of the medals in these unexpected places were signs from heaven that Margaret was both safe and still with them. It was a prayer of St. Margaret Mary seeking trust over fear that inspired the Leos to choose her name for their daughter. And now they were being asked to renew that trust, despite the profound sadness they were experiencing due to the loss of her physical presence.

The story of her brother Francis, whom she never met, bears the fragrance of Margaret. Margaret died on July 5, 2007. A few weeks later, on August 18, her brother Francis was conceived. This happened to be on the Feast of Saint Jane Frances de Chantal, Margaret's confirmation saint, though the Leos did not notice it at the time. Francis was named for St. Francis de Sales, the spiritual adviser to St. Jane de Chantal.

On Sally's second sonogram, the doctor noticed an abnormality. It appeared to be spina bifida. Subsequent tests showed it to be myelomeningocele, the most severe of the three forms of spina bifida and the *exact same kind* Margaret had. Film also showed Francis had what's called Chiari II malformation, a deformation of the brain that Margaret also had. It should be noted that it is exceedingly rare for this condition to visit the same family twice.

Sally made one simple request of Margaret. "It would be really great if he doesn't need a shunt." Subsequent sonograms, however, showed hydrocephalus, a sure sign he would eventually need a shunt. Sally felt challenged by this but was still willing to accept God's will. There was nothing else to do. Francis was delivered by C-section on May 5, 2008. Everything was then confirmed. He had exactly the same conditions as Margaret. It was also confirmed that he would need a shunt.

Surgery for the shunt was scheduled a few weeks later on May 13, the Feast of Our Lady of Fatima and oddly the anniversary of Margaret's first Communion. The procedure was successful. The shunt was in and working.

On June 6, however, Sally suspected the shunt was not functioning. Her new son's head had become enlarged. The doctor confirmed Sally's suspicions and surgery was scheduled for June 20. He was not yet in any danger. Sally, however, continued to pray to Margaret for her help with her little brother. She took Francis to Margaret's grave site to ask for her help.

The night before surgery, the Leos noticed his head no longer seemed enlarged; the soft spots on his head no longer seemed filled with spinal fluid. They suspected that the shunt was now working and that it had just been temporarily clogged. This was the best news of all. It is something that often happened to Margaret. When shunts get clogged, they might clear on their own or might need replacing. No matter what, though, the shunt was absolutely necessary to keep him alive.

The next day, the doctor examined Francis and determined that surgery was in fact no longer needed. All the symptoms had gone away. And then he discovered something remarkable: The shunt still wasn't working. It was still broken.

The doctor remarked, "Have you been praying or something?" He had never seen a case "where a baby with hydrocephalus after birth who is shunted no longer needs a shunt." A child may eventually grow out of needing a shunt but only in their teen years and beyond; he had never ever seen this in a baby. From that time to this day, Margaret's brother Francis has never needed a shunt.

Other blessings followed. The Chiari that so vexed Margaret—apnea, reflux, cognitive deficits, a cyst in the spine—and that Francis also has, has never caused him any problems at all. It's as if he has these problems but does not suffer from them. According to Margaret's doctors, she likely died because of a complication due to Chiari and a malfunctioning shunt.

Leonard says, "We don't know what all of this means, except that we're thankful to Our Lord for intervening, perhaps at Margaret's urging. After all, given her own situation in life, she'd certainly take quite an interest."

More fragrance of Margaret can be detected in the story of Ed Whelan's father. Whelan is an old friend and collaborator of Leonard's. He is president of the Ethics and Public Policy Center, an influential think-tank in Washington, DC. Whelan clerked for Justice Antonin Scalia, was general counsel to the Senate Judiciary Committee, and also served as principal deputy assistant attorney general for the Office of Legal Counsel at the Justice Department. In short, he has held senior positions in all three branches of the federal government.

Whelan is a deeply faithful Catholic and also quite precise in his public policy work. He is not given to excitation or exaggeration. He is certain the following story is real in every aspect.

It was the spring of 2007, only a few months before Margaret died. Leonard and Ed were up in New York attending the annual Becket Fund dinner, an event attended by conservative elites from around the country. Back in Northern Virginia, Ed's father attended a baseball game where he met Margaret for the first time. Ed says, "He apparently spoke with her quite a bit and was struck by her holiness." Without a doubt she talked to him about Jesus and the angels, and though bent over in her wheelchair, she was relentlessly happy. And she certainly wanted to know his birthday.

Ed's father came away saying he had met a living saint.

A few months after that meeting at the ballgame, on July 5, Margaret died. When informed of her death, Ed's father said, "She's surely in heaven." Less than two months later, Ed's father had a life threatening medical crisis. Ed explains, "On August 21, my father began suffering spasms and other severe symptoms—myoclonus jerking of the right hand and slurred speech—and was taken by ambulance to the emergency room." An EEG showed "epileptic form discharge and he was listed in critical condition."

According to Whelan and medical reports, on August 24 his father "showed a further decline in mental faculties (obtundation) and had a Glasgow coma score of 4." Those with a score of 3–8 are considered to be in a deep coma. An MRI brain scan showed "abnormal dura overlying the left partial area."

On Sunday, August 26, Whelan's mother called to tell him that his father "had suffered a serious decline. The doctors strongly suspected brain cancer or cancer that had spread to the brain." Doctors said Whelan's father might be on his deathbed. This was also the anniversary of Margaret's birth in 1992.

Ed emailed Leonard, "Our prayers are especially with you and your family on this anniversary of Margaret's birth. As it happens, I am leaving this afternoon for California, where my father is hospitalized with what appears to be, though testing isn't complete, brain cancer (or cancer that has spread from elsewhere to the brain). Remembering his warm recollection of his conversation with Margaret, I am praying for her intercession in bringing comfort to my father and to my mother."

Ed points out that from the time of her death only a month before, his family had added "especially St. Margaret Leo" at the conclusion of their invocations of all the saints at the end of their nightly prayers. He said years later that the family had been praying to Margaret since the beginning of his father's medical crisis.

Whelan says that upon their arrival in California, the doctors told the family that if their father lived, he would never have returned to an independent way of life. He would always have to be in assisted living. One of the doctors showed the family a picture of their father's brain and "how huge the growth was."

After Labor Day, new tests "stunned everyone." The growth on Ed Whelan's father's brain turned out to be dried blood. According to Ed, "My father was home shortly after that. Although his physical and mental capacities remain somewhat diminished, he is able to walk, drive, eat, talk, read, play cards, go to restaurants, go on vacations, and engage in the full range of activities that a typical eighty-year-old can engage in."

The Whelans consider his recovery a miracle for which they give credit to the newly deceased Margaret Leo.

And then there is the story of her brother Anthony's kidney. Prior to his senior year at The Heights, he lost a dramatic amount of weight. One day in August, at their vacation house in Maine, Anthony was too weak to get out of bed. At the hospital, they could not figure out the reason for his weight loss. In fact, they forgot all about it because they discovered he had only one kidney that was nearly in failure, a life-threatening condition.

They concluded later that his kidney problem was related to heavy intake of Ibuprofen—for headaches and baseball-related muscle pain—and antacids. What is the connection to Margaret? The Leos now believe she may have died from kidney failure due to heavy intake of both Ibuprofen during the long recovery period from the infection after the titanium rod surgery and antacids to relieve the terrible acid reflux brought on by one of her conditions.

Leonard explains that kidney failure is the silent killer. You don't know they are failing unless you have blood tests specific to that. In Margaret's case, they did not know. In Anthony's, his extreme weight loss led them to a blood test that happened to show his life-threatening kidney problem. They see Margaret's intervention in this. Interestingly, this happened to Anthony around Margaret's birthday.

Anthony was still a boy—only ten—when she died. It was not till much later that the impact of her simple faith hit him, but when it did, it hit hard. He thinks often of Margaret and the years they spent so close together. He is now studying philosophy at the Catholic University of America in Washington, DC. During his senior year in high school, he spent his afternoons studying at a Starbucks near his family's house. He recalls that, under her inspiration, he began to engage in open evangelization there. He says he talks about the Faith to anyone nearby; he especially likes talking to atheists. He told one young woman the story of the Sacred Heart Medals. She was a fallen-away Catholic. Her response to the story? She wept . . . and returned to the Church.

There are the smaller but no less significant things. Her funeral at the cathedral in Arlington was packed. This was due in no small part to the influence and network of her father, Leonard, but also to the fact that Margaret herself profoundly touched the people she met, and they wanted to pay their final respects. Given such a large crowd and the facts of Margaret's brief sojourn on earth, it is no surprise that people who might never have even met her walked away stunned after hearing the details of her short life. A cult of devotion grew up around her that day, one that still exists today.

Sally believes Margaret interceded for her at prayer one day. Margaret hated loud noise and for that reason did not care for birds. When they moved to the McLean house, Sally tried to put a bird feeder on the bedroom window, but Margaret said no, it would be too noisy. Windows had to be closed if there were noisy birds nearby.

Sally says she could not concentrate during adoration one day after her daughter's death at nearby St. John's church because the sparrows were making an awful racket. Sally said, "Margaret, I can't hear Jesus. Can you please ask God to tell those birds to go somewhere else?" And the birds immediately stopped. "It was kind of like wow, that was a surprise," Sally says today.

Margaret's effect on people is still manifest in the world today. A teacher at Oakcrest, the Opus Dei high school in nearby Vienna, Virginia, uses Margaret in one of her classes, just as a teacher at The Heights does with Brendan Kelly in his classes. Powerful men keep her picture in their wallets and on their desks and in their hearts and ask her for favors. Father Ed Hathaway says, "She was always cheerful among the great of Washington, DC," a circle of influence that included Supreme Court justices, senators, and even President George Bush. Leonard says it was amazing that someone so "ordinary could have such an extraordinary effect on other people."

He says, "She would remind people of a sense of humanity," something missing in the intense policy-driven world of Washington, DC and New York. He says in those cities, people tend not to pay close attention to each other, often looking around for the next person to see and be seen. "With Margaret," he says, "you would get her total attention. Nothing else would exist except for you."

Leonard puts it this way, "Hers is a story that people like to hear. People want to be like that. You want to be faced with rejection, you want to be faced with failure, you want to be faced with pain and with suffering and have her attitude. All of us would like that attitude anytime we are confronted with a situation we don't like. Wouldn't you like to be like that? Wouldn't you just like to say it's okay?"

It is not up to us to determine the authenticity of the birds stopping for Sally's prayer, or the healing of Ed Whelan's father, or the appearance of Sacred Heart Medals in odd places, or the curing of Anthony's kidney, or whether any of these events constitute instances of the miraculous, but we can recognize her inspiration in Anthony's life. We can see her inspiration in getting that young woman to return to the practice of the Faith. We can see her inspiration in Justice Thomas putting her picture on his desk at the Supreme Court, and we can see the cult that has spontaneously grown up around her. When I wrote a column about her three years ago at the website *The Catholic Thing* (www. thecatholicthing.org), we received more than one hundred requests for her prayer card from all over the world.

This, in the end, is the greatest part of Margaret Leo's story. She reached people and inspired them with her quick smile, simple questions, intense interest, and her simple love for God. Her brother Anthony said it best: "She loved the right things the right amount, simply and beautifully."

8

AUDREY OF LA CELLE SAINT CLOUD

FIVE thousand people listened to Mother Teresa in a great Parisian hall that autumn day in 1986. It was the first of its kind, a massive pro-family congress in Europe.

In the wings, waited a group of tiny children given the intimidating task of walking onstage in front of all those people and taking flowers to Mother when her talk was finished. When the time came, though, all of them quailed at the thought of walking out in front of such a massive crowd.

Seeing everyone's hesitation, tiny Audrey, then three years old, grabbed the flowers, sprinted onto the stage, and threw herself and the flowers into the arms of Mother Teresa. The crowd went crazy, a frenzy of clapping and cheering, a standing ovation.

Her mother, Lillian, says today, "That really was her personality." Exuberant, trusting, always determined, always rushing toward the things of the Faith. And as she rushed, she brought her family along with her.

Lillian was a casual, uncatechized Sunday Catholic, and her husband, Jerome, though Catholic, did not practice his faith regularly. Audrey was their second daughter. Lillian was born into a wealthy and socially-connected family. Her rather reserved, even remote, father was a banker, a fervent Sunday Catholic, albeit not engaged in the Catholic community in Chicago. Her mother—half-English, half-French—was Catholic but also influenced by her own Anglican mother. Even so, they knew enough to send Lillian to Catholic schools. Too bad for them and Lillian, this was in the 1960s and '70s when Catholic education fell apart and many classrooms became a place to lose the Faith rather than learn it.

Because Lillian's mother was part French, and they have extended family there, they packed her off to a girl's school in France. Lillian laughs when she says, "I arrived at the Catholic high school in France the year that all the nuns were leaving."

Lillian never came back to America to live. She eventually met a very handsome blond Frenchman with an English name. Jerome was born on La Réunion Island, and though he was raised Catholic, as were most in France at that time, he had ceased practicing. Lillian says, "I felt sure he would come back to the practice of the Faith."

Children came quickly: first Aline in 1981, then Audrey in 1983. More followed: Henry in 1985, Grégoire in 1987, and Beatrice in 1989. Lillian says in those days she was always looking to get more involved in the Faith. She says, "Jerome was not interested." Little did she know that the avenue through which that involvement would occur would be her own child.

In the midst of this lukewarm largely non-catechized family, Audrey nonetheless showed signs of a deep attraction to the Faith, even a supernatural attraction given someone so young. One day at Mass, she disappeared and was later found in the confessional. She told Lillian, "Mummy, there was a cross in there with Jesus on it. Just looking at Him, you love Him." Visiting the home of St. Thérèse of Lisieux, little Audrey said she wanted one day to enter "Caramel" rather than the proper term "Carmel." But all little girls say such things.

Because Lillian had been so badly catechized, she did not catechize her children very well. She says, for instance, she never taught her children about making sacrifices, not even during Lent, and so what Audrey did one day took her by surprise. "We were walking back from school, and I saw that she was sort of limping. And I said, 'Audrey, what's the matter, you're not walking properly.' I thought maybe she had put her shoes on the wrong foot. And so I stopped to look, and she didn't really want me to look inside her shoes, and I realized she had pencils in her shoes. I said, 'Well, Audrey, why do you have pencils in your shoes?'"

Audrey said, "It's much easier than carrying them, Mummy."

"Audrey, that's ridiculous; that's very uncomfortable."

And then Audrey said, "Je résiste (I resist)."

Lillian was stunned. Audrey had somehow learned mortification on her own, intuitively. No one taught her. She was four.

Lillian says, "That just became something she said often. 'Je résiste.' I would say to her, 'Audrey, why are you doing this or that?' and she'd just say, very quietly, 'Je résiste.' So she was sort of training herself, making herself give things up, or in this case really, a sacrifice."

And so it is not at all surprising in those early days that Lillian began to wonder, to ponder things in her heart, and even to fear. What was happening with her child? Where did little Audrey learn these wonders of the Faith that even adults did not know, and certainly did not practice? Not from Lillian or Jerome. Jerome was still largely non-practicing. Lillian was still no more than a Sunday Catholic, though she aspired to much more.

Lillian's reticence or even fear regarding her daughter's seemingly deep spirituality may perhaps be explained by the fact that she comes from a family where great and even deep reserve is highly treasured. Exuberant expressions, even of the Faith, especially of the Faith, do not seem to be a part of her family's DNA.

Moreover, France is a tricky place for the Faith. The French Revolution—with its widespread killing of priests and the general suppression of the Faith—is still celebrated each year on July 14, Bastille Day. The country has had imposed and now accepts the concept of laïcité, an almost rabid kind of secularism that chases religion from public policy, from the public square, and from much else. As a result, French Catholics are, in a sense, trained to keep their faith within certain accepted cultural bounds.

But Audrey did not seem to know that. She knew something else. She knew the exuberance of racing onto a stage in front of five thousand people and embracing a living saint. She knew the exuberance of making her little feet suffer so that she could resist the pain for love of God. No wonder Lillian was a bit frightened.

Lillian had signed Aline up for a children's prayer group that would pray for vocations. They were given a poster for vocations, "a very ugly poster," Lillian says, but one that Audrey made Lillian hang in the main room of the apartment. "She made the family assemble every evening to say this prayer in particular, plus then we added some others, ones I knew: Hail Mary, Our Father. And we said this prayer for vocations absolutely every day."

According to Lillian, Audrey had a way of saying, "I think it would be a good idea if we did this . . ." in a way "very gentle, but determined. And my husband and I would think, well, yes, it would be a good idea if we said prayers every evening with the children; she's right. And so we'd do it."

In addition to leading her family to prayer, Audrey had her own private devotions. Near the ugly poster for vocations, her parents had placed a statue of the Blessed Mother. "We would often find Audrey kneeling in front of the statue praying. She was very little. And sometimes in a very childish way, she'd get up and say, 'There, I've consoled her.' And just walk off to play."

Lillian says Audrey always gave away her sweets. "She would always go without," says Lillian. "In fact, it's embarrassing for me as a mother to say this, but it got to be so normal that Audrey would give things up—her toys, her desserts, whatever—for the others, that I didn't really realize that it was costing her. Sort of, 'Oh, yes. Well, here, Audrey, you'll give your share, won't you?' You know, like that. And I'd say, 'You didn't want it, did you Audrey?' But obviously she did."

Lillian and Jerome wondered who was teaching her. "Well, that's what was so disturbing for us as parents. We didn't know. Because she didn't, you know, go to catechism or anything; she couldn't read yet. That's why, at one point, what we said to Father Pierre, 'We feel very strange; it feels like somebody's just teaching Audrey things, and we don't know who it is.'"

The priest told Lillian and Jerome, "Follow her." And so they did.

It should be noted that Audrey was not a plaster saint. Audrey was the life of the party, the one who organized her friends at play.

She did have a great and proper sense of propriety, no doubt imbued from the greatly reserved genes she inherited from her mother's side of the family. Walking along a Parisian street one afternoon, she spied billboards with pictures of women on them and a phone number to call. Audrey referred to them as "ladies." And she said, "Mummy, let's pray for those ladies." Somehow she knew, even though she couldn't read, that there was something not quite right about those pictures.

She also sometimes balked at going to the birthday parties of other children because of what might be said there. She seemed determined to protect herself from the ugly things of the world, as if she was protecting her vocation to "Caramel."

In her biography of Audrey, Gloria Conde writes that Audrey "had been invited into the garden of the Beloved. Her soul, the soul of a child and of a woman hid itself in the cleft of the rock and rested there. There she drank from the wound in the side of her Beloved, and from there, she received her redemptive vocation."

There is something to this. She did seem to be set apart, given special graces, and—what is more—responded to them in ways well beyond her tender years.

At five, the determined little girl began lobbying her parents about receiving the Holy Eucharist. Five was too young in France, where children begin receiving at nine or ten. Lillian says, "That was very difficult because she just had it set in her mind she wanted to make her first Holy Communion, and she wanted to do it at Lourdes on August 15, the Feast of the Assumption."

Of course, they had to get special permission in order that one so young receive Communion. Even though the age of reception had been lowered many decades before, the acceptable age certainly wasn't five. Audrey's request did not require the bishop's approval, however, simply that of a priest, and so she was quizzed.

"What is Holy Communion?"

"Well, it's Jesus. And I want to receive Jesus."

Lillian says, "Some of these children have a sense, just a sense. And Audrey definitely did."

The trip to Lourdes was arranged, and on the day of her Communion Audrey was "just so unbelievably happy. It was just really sweet to see. She was so small. She was radiant. She was like a little queen." They had "a very small private Mass" where Audrey received for the first time but not before confessing for the first time, too. What in the world would five-year-old Audrey confess? It must have been profoundly beautiful, but we will never know.

Her first Communion, however, would not be the last time that Lourdes would play an important role in young Audrey's life.

Audrey's family lived in the Parisian suburb of La Celle Saint Cloud close by Versailles and not far from Normandy. The Normandy coast was where Audrey's family spent their idyllic summers—in a house purchased by Lillian's father for his French wife and as a place the family could gather every summer. Audrey loved it there. Their French cousins would come; so, too, her American family: Lillian's siblings, including her younger brothers McLean and Alexander.

McLean is now a priest, though he bounced in and out of seminaries in those days—uncertain of his vocation. He spent every summer, all summer long, in the Normandy house, so he knew Audrey well. He says she knew from the earliest age that "God is real and therefore everything that we do has to have relationship to Him."

McLean remembers to this day the prayer for vocations Audrey had the family say every night. In fact, he still says the prayer every day, and he has translated it into English, Russian, and Italian. The prayer is to Mary, the Mother of Priests. It includes the petition, "You have a special love for priests, because they are the living image of your son. Give us priests who will be saints." McLean says her insistence on this prayer is "a sign that she had this special supernatural insight into the mystery and the importance of vocations."

Alexander is perhaps even more reserved than his sister, Lillian. In those days, he was no more than a casual Catholic. Today he is an intense one, deeply involved with the things of the Faith. Alexander tells a story from those summers with the religiously precocious Audrey. She had instituted grace before meals. She had insisted upon it. The fact that she had to do so demonstrates how far her family was from the fervent faith they eventually would come to practice.

One day before lunch at the Normandy house, Audrey insisted on everyone saying grace, and Alexander, then a very young man, balked.

"Why, Audrey? Why do we have to say Grace before meals?"

"We have to thank Him for our food because He gave it to us."

"If He provided this food for us, then shouldn't we be thanking Him for everything all day long?

Without a moment's hesitation, Audrey said, "Of course we should."

Most of us strive mightily, if at all, to live in the presence of God. It is a difficult task for most of us. We learn tricks to remind us. We might leave a crucifix on the table to remind us. We might use triggers, like the ringing of a phone or the opening of a door, anything really, to remind us to make an aspiration, to place ourselves in His presence, anything to break out of the everyday tasks before us, those that take our entire attention and force our attention away from Him.

Others, like Audrey, seem to live in His constant presence with very little effort. They are imbued with His grace. They simply cannot forget. The story is told of St. Josemaría Escrivá that he was reading the newspaper one day and God intruded upon his thoughts and he said good-naturedly, "Can't I even read the newspaper?" Audrey was like that. She lived in His presence although she was only a child.

It was one summer's day—August, 1991—in idyllic Normandy when Audrey said she was too tired to go swimming. This is a shock to any parent that a child is too tired to go swimming. "She was always the first one in the swimming pool," says Lillian today. But that day, "she looked pale."

Lillian's mother-in-law said Audrey might be anemic and she should get a blood test, which Lillian thought unnecessary. Even so, she was tired in the middle of summer, pale, and perhaps a bit listless. They went for a blood test, and the doctors knew immediately: leukemia.

It should be noted that from very early on in Audrey's life, Lillian had a premonition of a great test coming for her daughter. She says today, "Just seeing the way she was developing, I mean spiritually, and the comments she would make, I got really frightened, because in spite of myself, I just suddenly thought there's something special about this child. I had so many examples of special children that something dreadful happened to. And I did get frightened. I thought, somebody with sort of that gifted spirituality . . . I just had this premonition. That was very disturbing."

She mentioned her fears back then to Jerome, and he rejected the notion. "Why do you think such things? That's dreadful," he said to her. But he came to agree. Once, Audrey got a terrible case of pneumonia and Lillian thought, "This is it, she's going to die of pneumonia." But she recovered.

That day at the doctor's office when the diagnosis came in, it all came flooding back. She called Jerome who was working in Paris, "Jerome, it's happened. It's leukemia.

And he knew immediately that what I meant was this thing, this great trial, this cross that we had been fearing."

A diagnosis of leukemia allows not a moment to waste. Leukemia can gallop through the blood and is a true emergency. The doctor told her to take Audrey to the hospital in Caen immediately.

The doctors told Lillian she had to tell Audrey she had leukemia, which Lillian thought was odd, but she was determined to do what the doctors advised, a notion she later rejected. In the meantime, she said to Audrey, "'You are very sick. It's a serious illness, and you are going to have to stay in the hospital.' Already this was odd because she had never spent a night away from home; she'd almost never been separated from me; she was only seven."

The stricken mother put on a brave face and told Audrey they would have to do everything the doctors told them to do, and if they did, she would get better. But Lillian says, "She got this very wise, very gentle sort of look. She looked out the window and said, 'Mummy, no. We're going to do what Jesus says. We're going to be like the birds in the sky. And we're just going to take one day at a time.'"

Lillian says, "I was floored. First of all, I didn't even know she knew that Gospel. I had no recollection of ever having read it to her. And even if I had at some point, that she would remember it, that she would refer to it. And that she had just immediately sort of knew how she was going to live this thing. And that stuck with us all through her illness, all through the year. And sometimes she would remind me, very gently."

"If I was worrying about some detail, the next day, how was I going to come to the hospital and take the children to school, and this and that, and whatever, and she would look at me with a little smile and say, 'Mummy, we'll worry about that tomorrow.' Yes, of course. Today we worry about today. And indeed, that was a great help to me. I think it was a help to Audrey, but it was particularly a great help to me. I mean, sometimes it was just living like ten minutes at a time. You know, you're thinking, 'Okay, if we can just get through these next ten minutes, she can be comfortable, she can be happy, make something nice. That will be good.'"

For, as Lillian realized, "In ten minutes, she might be dead." So with Audrey taking the lead, they endeavored to live ten minutes at a time.

Something happened to Jerome's twin brother on that same terrible day of the diagnosis that adds an aura of the supernatural to Audrey's sickness: A priest told him, "I see a great cross over your family that will be the source of many graces."

In spite of it all, Audrey never complained. She kept her pain and suffering to herself. "Je résiste. Je résiste." In fact, at the hospital that day, she admitted that her bones and joints had been aching for weeks before the blood test. But all throughout her sickness, they practically had to beg her to tell them how she felt. Doctors often say patients are the best doctors because they can describe what is happening to them. Audrey largely refused and instead offered it all up. "Offering it up" can be an empty phrase, sometimes tossed off without real meaning. Audrey didn't "offer it up" in such a fashion. She united her suffering with Christ on the Cross, and she did so for the conversion of sinners, for vocations, to make reparation for offenses against the Immaculate Heart of Mary. "There, I have comforted her." That is what Audrey did.

But Audrey also saw another, deeper meaning in her suffering. She said to Lillian, "I believe Jesus wants to remind me to be a good Carmelite."

Audrey began the treatments that would last a year until her death, only a year, twelve months for her family to live a whole lifetime with her. They did not know it at the time, they held out hope, but in the end it was only a year. But what a blessed year it was, living constantly in the shadow of death but always in the presence of God, living in a kind of hallowed land somewhere between heaven and earth.

Audrey was allowed to go home to La Celle Saint Cloud and thus began her treatment of blood transfusions and chemotherapy, which were done at a brand new children's hospital called Robert-Debré—less than twenty miles away but nonetheless a penitential slog through Parisian traffic.

The hospital was truly foreign territory to Lillian and Audrey. First, Lillian says the doctors did not explain anything to them. Even worse than that, the doctors and nurses assiduously avoided bonding with Audrey because the emotions attached to such bonding could become horribly painful if she died, which was a real possibility for all of the children in that ward. In fact, hospital personnel were forbidden to establish personal relationships with the patients. Lillian said the lack of human contact was especially painful for Audrey. "She couldn't understand why, and we obviously could not tell her the reason." Later, near the end when Audrey was taken to Lourdes, she brought back a religious medal for one of the nurses who was Catholic. She was not allowed to give the medal to the nurse.

This cold, distant treatment was such that there was no one to plump her pillow, no one to help her with her food. Audrey once badly burned herself when, on her own, she tried to open a dish of hot food that spilled onto her stomach.

And then there was the improper flirting that happened between and among the hospital personnel. Audrey could hear them in the hallway and it troubled her deeply. Audrey really did think she was headed for a Carmelite vocation, and so she endeavored to protect herself from anything on the street, on television, and at birthday parties that would adversely affect her vocation. Even her constant attempts at mortification—pencils in her shoes, giving away her candy, her desserts—can be seen as the little girl preparing herself not for death (how would she know that?) but for her lifelong commitment to a vocation to "Caramel."

Though Audrey was troubled by the flirting of the hospital staff, perhaps even more difficult than that for the family—albeit something she herself perhaps did not even notice, though Lillian did—was the overt anti-Catholicism in the hospital. The hospital was a secular one in a France that is secular to the point of outright hostility to the Faith. "They definitely did not like the fact that we were Catholic, that Audrey had a little statue of Mother Mary in her room." Lillian says she hid the anti-Catholicism from Audrey. "That's just too complicated for a child to deal with."

Treatment for Audrey was nothing short of harrowing. There were frequent spinal taps. And they were undertaken in that impersonal way that made them even more harrowing. Lillian says that all of a sudden masked doctors and nurses would appear in Audrey's room and, without warning or a word, flip her over and administer the very painful tap. This would often happen when Lillian was not present.

Lillian told them, "We're not doing this anymore. This is not how we are doing this with Audrey. We'd like to know before, and I would like to be there." Lillian says, "Audrey wanted to know before because she wanted to prepare herself, but mostly so as to decide who she was going to offer this up for. What intention. And it was always for religious vocations. That was really Audrey's thing. Like little Thérèse of Jesus, she loved so much. Always for vocations." And incidentally, it should be noted, for her father's chain-smoking.

Audrey was diagnosed on August 8, 1990. She was treated on an outpatient basis from then until the end of October. Word spread of her suffering and her closeness to God, and so the prayer requests began, dozens of them, knocks on the door, slips of paper handed to Jerome or Lillian. "Please ask Audrey to pray for me, my father, mother, sister, daughter," things to that effect. Audrey was sanguine about them, though at times overwhelmed. At one point she suggested to Lillian that they put them in a basket and pray for them all at once. But she thought better of it. "I will pray for each one of them."

And so the little girl prayed . . . and suffered. October came and nothing was working; sixty days of treatment had not worked. Audrey was not getting better. Her blood counts were still awful, horrible, cancerous. And so at the end of that October, Audrey was admitted to the hospital where she lived for the next six and a half months.

Her time there was one long way of the cross. She suffered almost constantly from either loneliness, not being able to see the sky or feel the sun on her face, the impersonal treatment from the doctors and nurses, the pain of injections and tests, or the humiliation of being prodded and examined both clothed and, embarrassingly, unclothed. The chemotherapy made her sick and she vomited all the time, though she did not tell her mother.

But as with Christ on the Cross, this helpless girl offered it all for others. Constant was her pain and even more constant were her prayers for others.

When the aggressive chemotherapy began, her mother told her that her beautiful hair would fall out. Audrey said she would be the first nun in France to offer her hair not once but twice to Christ. In solidarity, her sister Aline cut off her own hair too. Audrey might have been largely alone except for the constant visits of her mother, but she was lifted up in prayer at home and also around Versailles. A Tuesday night Rosary began for Audrey that eventually spread around France.

A prayer card was created that used the first letters of Audrey's name as an acrostic. The card went around the world. Audrey's godmother said she was approached by a woman in a Lyonnaise church asking her to pray for a little girl suffering in Paris from leukemia. She wept when she saw the woman hand her Audrey's prayer card.

Something dramatic was happening as this little girl lay dying in a Parisian hospital. There were many children suffering the same fate in the same hospital and others around the world, but it was Audrey that caught the religious imagination of people all over the world. Whole convents of nuns prayed for Audrey.

Even in these harrowing months, great graces and even seeming miracles occurred. One day they gave Audrey a particularly heavy dose of chemo, and her body reacted badly. In great pain, Audrey's system simply crashed. As it happened, two priests had come to the hospital to offer Audrey the anointing of the sick. When they touched her forehead with the Holy Oil, she grew calm and her system revived.

The nights, however, were perhaps the worst. She was alone, hooked up to machines, the door opened slightly, and she could hear the offensive flirting and gossip going on among the staff. Audrey prayed, "Help them. Forgive them. Protect me."

One doctor took to calling Audrey "my little bunny," and she hated it. She also hated that he pinched the nurses and called them similar names, his impure intentions clear. Audrey made it clear that she did not want him as her doctor, and so he was replaced. Lillian intervened. She corrected her daughter, saying he acted that way because he did not know Christ. He had never been told a better way.

Audrey not only relented but also asked for him to return and apologized to him, and from that day forward, she was exceedingly kind to him. She prayed for him every day. She explained the Mass to him. Later, when she had to enter the sterile bubble, she asked for him.

Audrey was a tiny child. The chemo fatigued her, made her nauseous, caused sores to open in her mouth, dried her saliva, and made her eyelids stick to her eyes. Her bones ached. Audrey repeated over and over, "I am on the cross. I am on the cross." She was uniting her suffering to His on the Cross. He was not on the Cross alone. She was with Him, her beloved, and she suffered with Him; she offered her suffering for the redemption of others.

One of those praying for her was Pope John Paul II. After the first of the year, 1991, Jerome took the other children—Aline, Beatrice, Henry, and Grégoire—to Rome to witness priestly ordinations in St. Peter's and to pray for Audrey. Little boys being little boys, Greg had to pee at the most inopportune moment. Jerome had to talk his way through a number of guards to get Greg to the men's room inside the massive basilica. They were back in their seats only a few minutes when Greg started up. He had to go again. Frustrated, Jerome brusquely snatched him up and went back the same way to the men's room, and this time, he ran smack into an old friend of his who was in the Swiss Guard, a colonel no less. Single-minded Jerome pressed his friend to get them into John Paul II's private Mass so he could ask the pope to pray for Audrey. For faithful Catholics, few experiences this side of heaven can match that: to attend the private Mass with the pope and then to be greeted by him afterward. His friend said it was a long shot, but he would try. Jerome's frustration with Grégoire faded into kisses for the surprised boy.

His friend's efforts were successful, and the next day, they were directed to the "Bronze Doors", massive double doors up huge steps on the right side of St. Peter's Basilica guarded by two elaborately uniformed members of the Swiss Guard. This is the door that leads to the pope's private apartment and chapel. After Mass, Jerome pressed Audrey's prayer card into the pope's hand, who bent forward and heard her story from the aggrieved father who only a few years before was not even practicing the Faith. Pope John Paul II said, "Audrey. Audrey. Yes, we will pray for her."

The months passed. January turned to February, which turned to March, and no improvement came in Audrey's condition. At one point, in fact, she went blind as a result of the chemotherapy. It did not last, but while she was blind, she told no one, not even her mother. She faked it and offered her blindness up. She only admitted she was blind when Lillian caught on while they "watched" television one day.

Ultimately, with nothing working, a bone marrow transplant was decided upon. This was practically the end. In preparation, they placed her in a sterile bubble where she would stay for six weeks, without human contact, not able to touch or be touched by her mother. Doctors touched her only with special gloves.

A bone marrow transplant is an operation in which your bone marrow is taken completely from your body and replaced with someone else's, in Audrey's case, her brother Henry's. Before that comes radiation. Hours of radiation, lying in a sterile room all alone. In the little room all alone, Audrey could be heard singing songs to God, to Mary, and saying Aves. Everyone could hear her, doctors and nurses included, singing her little hymns of love.

Audrey was connected to tubes: tubes for everything, tubes for medicine, tubes for food, tubes for water. The transplant was done on March 8. Audrey's only concern was young Henry. He was not used to hospitals, and she was worried about him.

And then the wait began, the waiting and watching for her blood count to rise. That is the marker that things have gone well and that she at least had a chance that her new blood would multiply and that it would not be rejected by her body and that the cancer would be defeated.

Good Friday came on March 29 that year and things were looking up. Her blood count was improving. It was the only good news they had received since her diagnosis seven long months before. But on that day, Audrey had a crisis. She felt a massive pain in her chest, and she said, "It's my heart. It's my heart." Audrey fell back on her pillow and made the Sign of the Cross over and over above her chest. Lillian thought she was having a heart attack and called for the nurse, who came running. The cardiogram showed her heartbeat had declined nearly to nothing, as if she were dead or dying. And then she revived. The crisis passed. Lillian looked at her watch. It was 3 p.m., the time that Christ died on Good Friday. Three p.m., the time that is known as the Hour of Mercy.

On April 15, with her blood count up and her immune system seemingly stable, she was moved out of the sterile bubble into a regular room and began physical therapy to restore the inevitably atrophied muscles, therapy designed to make her strong enough to move to a rehabilitation center. The family was thrilled and began to make plans to make a visit of thanksgiving to Lourdes, a cautious celebratory lap where precocious Audrey had received first Holy Communion just a few years before.

But she didn't get better. She wasn't getting stronger. She was becoming listless again. At first the doctors said this was the result of her months of treatment. Her full discharge was coming up on May 12, and they ran one more test on the anniversary of the first appearance of Our Lady at Fatima.

The news devastated Lillian and Jerome. The doctors gave Audrey only weeks to live. They offered her an experimental procedure, but Lillian and Jerome declined. She could have stayed in the hospital until the end, but they decided to take her home so that she could pass away in her own room surrounded by family and friends and near their home chapel where the bishop allowed them to keep the Blessed Sacrament.

At the hospital, Lillian broke the news to Audrey that they were taking her home. Audrey said, "But aren't they going to put me in the recovery house?"

"No, Audrey. The transplant didn't work. We're going home." Just the thought of saying that to your sick daughter and the implications are enough to make the angels quake and cry.

Audrey told her mother, "We are going to live like the birds of the sky. One day at a time."

And so Jerome and Lillian took their daughter home.

Even those final days were not wasted. Nothing with Audrey was ever wasted. While her own marrow was poisoned with cancer, she nonetheless sucked the marrow out of every living moment she could, living constantly immersed in God.

Jerome and Lillian had already considered taking something of a victory lap at Lourdes, that is, when Audrey's blood count seemed to improve. They decided to go anyway, though now on a different kind of journey, a different kind of victory lap.

Audrey was excited to be going to Lourdes, to the place she received her first Communion. She was terribly sick, terribly weak. She was in a wheelchair, a mask on her face, her bloated head covered in a red bandanna, nearby a huge bag of medicine she had to take every day. What's more, she had to have a complete blood transfusion every few days. So the trip would be a whirlwind.

At the airport, Audrey was recognized. She had appeared in a documentary on the new children's hospital. "Isn't that the girl from television?" one little boy asked.

When they arrived, Lourdes was immersed in cold rain and fog. It was May, bad weather being quite typical for that time of year. The town lies fallow for half the year, and the pilgrim season had not yet begun, so a priest-friend got a local hotel to open just for Audrey and her family. On this trip, she was accompanied by Lillian and Jerome, of course, Audrey's godmother Brigitte, Jerome's twin brother Marc, Aline, and Uncle Mick, who had flown in from the States.

The next morning after Mass, they went down to the baths at the grotto for the immersion. Lillian prepared Audrey and told her, "We are going to pray to Mary. We are going to put in her hands the intention we carry in the depths of our hearts. And we are also going to pray for you to be cured."

As always, Audrey's prayers were directed away from herself, "Mummy, I already know what I'm going to offer my bath for. It's for a young man who is doubting his vocation." It was a young man she heard about in the hospital.

Imagine those quiet moments in nearly deserted Lourdes: the soft rain, gray clouds, the silence of the stones, the hushed prayers even in the hotel. They knew that these moments could very well be their last with her. She could go at any time. Graces piled upon graces in Lourdes during these final days.

The family flew back to Orly Airport outside Paris, and upon landing, Jerome asked his dying daughter the wildest thing. "Do you want to go to Rome?"

"Oh yes, very good," she said. Audrey said she had been hoping for some time to go to Rome and, in particular, to visit the prison where Peter and Paul were held. What an odd thought for such a child.

They left for Rome immediately without even going home. It was as if they were in a race to fill her final days, their final moments together, with graces and memories.

Jerome called his friend Colonel Aloïs of the Swiss Guard and begged to attend the pope's private Mass once more, this time with Audrey. He said he would try. But first, they had to see the Mamertine Prison where the Romans held Peter and Paul. Rome is among the least wheelchair friendly cities in the whole world. Nothing but cobblestones, and the sidewalks can be an uneven mess. And that is the modern part of Rome. The Roman Forum is impossible, the tiny prison, even worse. Jerome and Uncle Mick carried the wheelchair and Lillian carried tiny feather-light Audrey in her arms down the steep soft worn-away steps. Aline carried Audrey's bag of medicine.

Audrey wanted to go all the way in, all the way down, and so they went down even more precarious steps, down to where Peter and Paul were held below ground, water trickling down the walls, humid cold stones all around, down to the altar set against a wall. What could have gone through Audrey's mind down there? Peter and Paul sitting right there chained to the wall would have been as real to her as her mother and father, Aline, and Uncle Mick, and in her little insightful precocious mind, she likely saw a straight unbroken line extending from Peter and Paul sitting there long ago to herself at that moment being held in her mother's arms.

Aloïs called. The private Mass with John Paul II was arranged for the next morning. But only four people would be allowed to go. Jerome remembers this as practically the only time he ever scolded Audrey, because Audrey insisted that she not go and that Uncle Mick go in her place. Mick was dithering about his vocation to the priesthood. He had tried two seminaries and had left them both. He tried his hand at Hollywood, too, writing scripts. She was sure that was not for him. She was sure that his life's vocation was to the priesthood and just as sure that seeing the pope might help make this clear to Mick. But Jerome put his foot down. It was going to be four: Lillian, Jerome, Aline, and Audrey. Mick would stay behind. But Audrey negotiated a deal in return. Aline promised to ask the pope to pray for Mick's vocation.

The Holy Father's "right-hand man," Monsignor Stanisław Dziwisz, greeted them at the elevator and took them to the chapel where four chairs were waiting just for them. Four nuns had given up their seats and were standing in the back. Everyone knew the little girl in the wheelchair was dying.

After Mass they were ushered into the nearby library to greet the pope personally. John Paul II bent down to speak with Audrey. His arms around her, their faces touched, hers swollen and bloated, her bald head covered in that red bandanna. They spoke quietly together for several minutes. What they shared is not known, but knowing the little girl and the great man, there can be little doubt that it was simple yet profound, something about vocations and her love for Jesus and Mary and nothing, not a word, about her suffering. Did she teach him something about suffering that prepared him for his own? At the Vatican that day, he said her name over and over, "Audrey, Audrey, Audrey."

Flustered young Aline forgot to ask the Holy Father for his prayers for Mick's vocation, but Audrey said not to worry, at that moment, she asked Jesus to speak to the pope about it.

On the plane ride home, Lillian said to Audrey, "You have been held by Mother Teresa and now the pope. What more could you want?"

"For Jesus to hold me in His arms." They all knew that would be soon. What a blessing it was for Audrey finally to go home. She had been in the hospital for all of the previous seven months. Now she was in her own bed with the view of the front garden and the tree just outside, with the new wallpaper of little yellow ducks she had chosen herself. She laid her head on her own pillow in her own room in her own house. What a blessing.

Lillian was told she had to prepare Audrey for the inevitable, as if the precocious little one did not know. "You know, Audrey, that if a day comes when you have to go to heaven before me, I am sure that you will find your true mother there. She will take very good care of you—you'll see—because she loves you much more than I ever could." To this day, Lillian remembers practically word for word everything Audrey said that final year. She says it was a special kind of blessing. It is as if Lillian was an apostle soaking up every word, never to forget, so as to be always able to tell others, to pass along the story. And so Lillian remembers most clearly what Audrey said in response to her talk of her beloved daughter finding her true mother in Mary, the Mother of God, "Ah yes, I know that very well."

She knew it very well. She knew the Blessed Mother was waiting for her and Jesus, too. This is the girl who, at the age of five, was able to explain the Eucharist so she could get special permission to begin receiving Communion four or five years early. "Ah yes, I know that very well." Very well indeed.

Audrey spent as much time as she could in those final weeks in the small chapel in front of the tabernacle that the local bishop allowed them to have at their home. It was then, too, that the stream of visitors began. People knocked on the door constantly. They wanted to see her, pray for her, but more than anything, to ask for her prayers. They knew she was immersed in God and that God was immersed in her.

Her grandmother asked her one day what she did when she woke up in the morning. "I pray and I wait." Praying and waiting; doesn't that sum up the life of a Carmelite?

And what a lot of waiting Audrey did in that last year. Lying in her hospital bed unable to move, hour upon hour, waiting for Lillian, waiting for the doctor, waiting for the sun, waiting for Christ.

Just as she had desired early Communion, so she desired early Confirmation, at least in terms of the standard age for the sacrament. In those final days, Audrey wanted to be confirmed, and she wanted a big party, too. She was determined, and it was allowed.

She wanted it to be "elegant." That was one of her favorite words. "Elegant" not in the sense that Park Avenue socialites might employ the term, but rather in the way that the Blessed Mother would use it: simple, true, beautiful, perfect . . . elegant. Audrey helped choose everything for that party, and she spent hours arranging and rearranging. She chose the holy cards to mark the occasion, and she signed and dated each one. Her uncle Mick watched her and marveled. He marvels to this day. Even today you can see the joy on his face as he remembers that June day twenty-five years ago.

Having been confirmed and having had her "elegant" party, still Audrey hung on. Jerome and Lillian tried to keep things as normal as possible. They lived near the Palace of Versailles, so they would go there for picnics. The Capuchin priests of Versailles said Mass for the end of the school year and Audrey asked to go; she was overjoyed to see her friends. "Mummy, I saw my friends." How sweet that was because they were fairly new to La Celle Saint Cloud when she got sick and then she was gone, lost behind the impenetrable wall that surrounds the land of the sick. But in her short time with them, she made such an impression. She was the one who gave away all her treats and shared her lunch.

Still, new crosses continued to come. One day Audrey convulsed. Her eyes rolled back and her body shook. Over and over this would happen for most of that night, her mother lying near her, stroking her arm and speaking softly to her. Finally, Audrey fell asleep. When she awoke, her hands were clenched. She could not control her eyes, and one hand jumped up and down. "It's like a frog," Audrey said with her usual humor, making light of this new cross. In the coming days, Audrey struggled to regain the use of her gnarled hand so she could at least scrawl. Lillian says, "She would force herself to hold her pen and to make her letters."

It was summer. A hot July gave way to an even hotter August, the time when all of France goes on a month-long vacation. The whole family would gather each year at the house at Maillot in Normandy, the one Lillian's American banker-father bought for his French wife. Everyone came every year, the far-flung family from France and the United States. It was a part of their lives, and this year was no different in that sense but oh so different in another.

Lillian says, "That was a real time of grace. That was beautiful. Well, she was very, very ill, of course. She couldn't get out of bed anymore. I took her back to Normandy because you see; it was the summertime by then. And all my family were in Normandy, and for her little brothers and sisters, it would be nice for them to be in the country during the summer. And every summer we had been to Normandy, so for Audrey it was sort of the thing to do. So I took her to Normandy; my husband stayed in

Paris because he was working. And Audrey was very ill, she couldn't get out of bed . . . hardly—or sometimes I'd carry her, like to go visit the farm next door that she loved very much, with the little rabbits and all that. But she was very ill. She really would spend her time in bed, praying. We had a priest who was a neighbor who came to visit her almost every day, said Mass, heard her confession; she wanted to go to confession very often. She would pray. That's when she started hearing these voices."

Lillian heard her talking to someone even though the room was empty: "Oh, yes. Well, thank you. Oh, thank you, thank you for answering me so soon." Was it Mary? Was it Jesus?

Even in these final days and weeks, Audrey kept up her prayer intentions, the basket of requests having grown to a torrent. Lillian says, "So it goes through this long list. And for people who she didn't really know. For so-and-so, and this and that, and all these different things. And she thought it was very important to pray each intention especially to 'Her Lord,' as she called Jesus—'Mon Seigneur'—to take care of these intentions."

And she prayed especially for her beloved uncle Mick whom she knew had a vocation to the priesthood. Now Father McLean, he recalls the day he sat with her in the Normandy house explaining that he was going to Rome to enter his third seminary. He says, "I remember her just sort of putting up her hand and saying, 'I know it's difficult.' It really struck me later as this example of the gift of wisdom, that the Holy Spirit had taught her all about discernment. It seemed to me she had so much maturity and experience that she knew how difficult discernment is. There was no need to say more. It was really beautiful. She put me totally at ease. I had the sense that she totally understood, and then I had the confidence that now everything would go smoothly, which it did."

One day not long after, she asked for Uncle Mick, "Where is he? Where is he?"

Lillian told her, "Audrey, McLean has left; he's gone to Rome. He's gone to the seminary."

"Oh, then I can rest!" she exclaimed and slipped back into unconsciousness. And those were practically Audrey's last words on earth. She could finally rest.

Sensing the very end was upon them, the family took Audrey back to their house in La Celle Saint Cloud, to her own little room with the yellow ducks and the tree outside. Lillian sat by her bedside and waited; Audrey was in and out of consciousness, mostly out. Lillian wet her lips with Lourdes water and Audrey said, "Thank you, Mummy." Her last words. She passed away that afternoon at three o'clock, the hour of mercy, the hour of Christ's death. It was August 22, 1991, the Feast of the Queenship of Mary. Jerome had prayed that when Audrey was taken, it would be on a day dedicated to the Blessed Mother.

Audrey had a profound effect on her family. Their spiritual life deepened in profound ways, and three of her siblings entered religious life. Jerome and Lillian both work on Church-related projects. Jerome helped found the global Catholic website Aleteia.org. Lillian was secretary general of the World Union of Catholic Women's Organizations and has run conferences at the Vatican.

Though not canonized or beatified, devotion has grown up naturally and organically around Audrey's memory among those who knew her and many many others around the world. Seminaries still pray to Audrey for her intercession for vocations. The convent of Carmelites located in the legendary palace at El Escorial in Spain, home of the Spanish kings and queens, requested an article of clothing from Audrey. The family gave them her first Holy Communion dress. It hangs there still, in the chapter hall, framed under glass.

And not to be unexpected perhaps, the Audrey "stories" have not stopped. There was a young man from Brazil who also suffered from leukemia. Deeply depressed, he decided to commit suicide. A priest told him about a little girl in Paris who was suffering right then from the same thing and that she offered all her pain to God. This is how far and how fast the story of Audrey spread, even while she was alive. The young man considered that, and Audrey's story helped him through the darkest of times.

Some years later, the young man came to France to work for the Church. Audrey's family opened their home for such people as they came into France, a way station on the way to apostolate. The young man told his story to Jerome: leukemia, thoughts of suicide, and how he was saved by the example of a little girl in Paris.

Jerome said, "That girl was Audrey, and you're sitting on her bed."

9

LESSONS OF THE LITTLEST
SUFFERING SOULS

WHAT can we learn from these little holy ones who seemed to have a more direct connection to God, a more real experience of the supernatural? What strikes you first about their stories is not just how much they suffered but the way in which they did so: with a grace and strength rare even among the most spiritually advanced adults, let alone children.

Audrey's parents had to order her to talk about her pain so they and the doctors could help. Margaret would rarely mention her pain and mostly smiled through it. In the deepest pain, Brendan tried to make his parents laugh so they would not worry about him. Most children are not like this. We adults aren't like this.

We humans strive to avoid pain. We mask it with ever-improving pain relievers. We take to our beds. We whimper and complain. We talk about our pain, perhaps every day. A friend's casual "How are you?" can invite a recitation of the most minor annoyances and aches. Perhaps some of us, some of the time, think to offer it up as we Catholics should, but doing so is not easy.

Suffering is one of the great mysteries. As a subject for contemplation, it has occupied not only the greatest minds of all time but others as well, yours and mine, for instance.

One of the Four Noble Truths of Buddhism includes suffering and how to use the Noble Eightfold Path to avoid it. Hinduism sees suffering as a kind of punishment for bad behavior. Islam says the faithful must endure suffering as a test of faith.

Only Christianity, and particularly Catholicism, sees suffering as redemptive, as a way to share in the suffering of Christ on the Cross, to lessen His pain, and to complete His redemption, as John Paul taught us. Catholics also believe suffering can be offered for the good of others. This notion is utterly foreign to most faiths, and even scandalous to our Protestant brothers and sisters.

Upon hearing Audrey's story, one woman said she simply could not fathom the idea that Audrey's story could be true. She warned that adults sometimes impose certain ideas upon young people and wondered if Audrey's parents imposed a kind of early religiosity on her. The woman, who is not Catholic, wondered if adults sometimes see things in children that are not really there. You can see how that could be the case. In fact, it is good, even essential, for Catholics to retain a healthy skepticism, properly understood, about alleged religious phenomena.

The stories you have just read involve no such dramatic, whether authentic or not, miraculous occurrences. No weeping statues. No stigmata. Only normal children in extraordinary circumstances. They were children first and foremost, not objects of religious imaginations. None of them wanted to be sick or to suffer.

Brendan was the life of the party. I have seen pictures of him dancing at weddings with friends and family cheering him on. He loved sports. Audrey may have had an acute sense of propriety, shying away from some birthday parties because of bad words she might hear there, but still she was a normal little girl who played with her sisters and her friends. Margaret loved to watch other children play in the park. They were normal everyday children who happened to be given great crosses as well as tremendous graces.

So what can we learn from them? What is God trying to tell us through their example?

Clearly, forbearance is one lesson. Audrey practiced forbearance even before the onset of physical suffering. "Je résiste." Something inside of her, something deep within her soul, some force, perhaps supernatural, helped her to prepare for what came later.

Brendan and Audrey, who suffered intense and long-lasting pain, offered their pain for others, and they knew what they were doing. And they did not merely or perfunctorily "offer it up." They united their suffering with Christ on the Cross to help Him complete the Redemption. Perhaps they would not have put it that way, but somehow that is precisely what they were doing.

Shouldn't we remember these lessons the next time we bump our heads on an open cabinet door or the next time someone cuts us off in traffic? How about some minor inconveniences that can send us around the bend? Let us always remember those bent titanium rods in Margaret's back now found on her father's desk. As they remind him of what a bad day really looks like, let them remind us.

Simplicity is another lesson. Neither Brendan nor Audrey nor Margaret were complicated people. Alvaro de Vicente of the Heights School says Brendan had a "simplicity of soul. There were no folds. There was nothing that would make his personality or his soul incompatible with anyone else's." The same could be said for Audrey and Margaret. That is something to ponder about each of these children and the three children with whom we began the book; the consideration of this should encourage each of us to simplify ourselves, too. Don't we live in a remarkably complicated world, one that we can make even worse by the complications we bring to it? Simplicity, transparency, a lack of guile; these are needed in this day and age of suspicion and widespread lack of trust.

We can learn from these children a greater love of the Eucharist. Did you notice that each of these children loved the Eucharist and knew what, or rather Whom, it was, knew intensely? Audrey begged to receive when she was five, well before she ever got sick. She begged to have the Blessed Sacrament in her house as she lay dying. Margaret was solemn and silent at the consecration of the Sacred Host and profoundly contemplative after reception when she would simply say, "Thank you for coming to me in Communion today." And then there is Brendan. When he was home in a sterile bubble and no one could touch him, he asked to be taken to the parking lot of the church so that Father Drummond could walk down the center aisle during Mass and out the front door of the church so that he could receive the Eucharist through an open window of the big black Suburban. How often do we receive Christ without thinking, certainly without contemplation? These children who, though they came from wealthy families and did not lack for anything in one sense, did lack the most basic blessing of all that most of us take for granted: good health. And yet, lacking that, they possessed a treasure that so many of us cannot be bothered with. They possessed Christ.

Perhaps a lesson for us and for the Church is that even, perhaps especially, children can aspire to live the virtues to a heroic degree. Did not Christ say that we must become like little children? While we do not sanctify these children in this book, we recognize and may be permitted to hope and pray that the Church may one day do so.

But are there even larger lessons we can learn from them? What can we learn from the fact that they were born into great spiritual deserts, not within their own families, but in the larger social and professional milieu where their families resided? These three children were not shepherd children. They were the children of the vastly influential, but there are few places more spiritually arid than the policy world of Washington, DC or modern France, as anyone who has spent any time in either place knows.

Yet these children were given these great spiritual gifts in these particular social circumstances at this precise time for a reason. The story of their lives must become widely known, especially to inhabitants of those influential deserts where they were born, those making policy, and those manufacturing opinions from their perches in the media and the academy, precisely because the so-called "elites" have always had a powerful impact on society. This fact, that of the influence of the "elites," is evident from Scripture and all we know about history. Consider also that it is through the influence of the "thought leaders," the "elites," and not from the man in the street that the most profoundly troubling ideas related to human sexuality have become widely accepted.

Could it be that these three children—born to influential families, born into the vast desert of societal elites—were sent as a message of purity and innocence to those self-same elites? And that in a divine carom shot, a recovered elite would act as an example to the poor? Is this the way God walks back the sexual revolution, through the example of these and perhaps others still to come of the littlest suffering souls?

But there is an even larger lesson to be learned from these brave little souls, a meta-lesson, if you will. It is a lesson in a grand battle the Church has been fighting at least from the time of the Enlightenment: It is nothing less than a battle for the human person, which may be considered the great fight of the modern age.

It is no surprise that the great defender of the human person in our time was and still is Pope Saint John Paul the Great, who can be considered the *Theologian of the Human Person*. Through writings beginning with *Love and Responsibility*, published in 1960 only two years after he was named auxiliary bishop of Krakow, extending through the documents of the Second Vatican Council, in which he played a prominent role, and culminating in the documents of his pontificate such as *Centesimus Annus* (1991), *Veritatis Splendor* (1993), *Evangelium Vitae* (1995), and so many other encyclicals, sermons, and exhortations, John Paul II again and again came to the rescue of the human person over against all the ideologies of the Modern Age.

Perhaps we may be excused if we discern the hand of Providence in the fact that John Paul came into contact with two of our little suffering souls. It is quite remarkable that he had close contact and private conversations with both Audrey and Brendan. Even now in your mind's eye, you can see him leaning down, taking their faces in his hands, and exchanging soft words. For that matter, we don't have to rely on our mind's eye, as a simple search for the images online will allow you to see them for yourselves.

Perhaps he remembered these little ones and even drew strength from their suffering; perhaps they served as a model for him when, towards the end of his own life, he came to suffer greatly in a long and drawn-out, yet supremely edifying, public way of the cross. He showed us how to suffer, to carry our suffering with dignity, and he showed us how to die.

People see someone like John Paul II in his final agony—shaking hands, slurred, almost unintelligible speech—and wonder if this is a life worth living.

They see a child with Down syndrome and do not see a human person. Ninety percent of them who are seen in utero are aborted. Their lives are considered by so many today to be not worth living. They do not meet our flawed modern expectations and conceptions of what constitutes human dignity. Modern man sees a child with spina bifida—all hunched over in a wheelchair, having to be wheeled everywhere—as a wasted life and, what is worse to his way of thinking, wasted resources. Such a man, if he can be called such, might experience more wonderment at the sight of a robot than in this child of God. Our modern man might see a child suffering from leukemia who has died young and see nothing but a misbegotten tragedy, a life with no meaning.

In the simplest terms, modern man is wrong. The *Littlest Suffering Souls* stand as witnesses to the proposition that all human life has meaning and dignity, even and especially those lives we may not fully understand. Indeed, each of them in their short lives so full of suffering achieved more than the richest Silicon Valley billionaire who may have done great things and amassed great wealth in the eyes of the world but who has lived for nothing if he lived for anything other than the love of neighbor and the love of God.

Little Nellie of Holy God, Venerable Antonietta Meo, Mary Ann Long, Brendan Kelly, Margaret Leo, and Audrey lived heroically for God and neighbor, and that, in the end, is why we will remember them, indeed why the Church may never forget them.

BIBLIOGRAPHY

Books

Anonymous. *The Life of Little Nellie of Holy God: The Little Violet of the Blessed Sacrament.* Charlotte: TAN Books, 2009.

Conde, Gloria. *Audrey: The True Story of One Child's Heroic Journey of Faith.* North Haven, CT: Circle Press, 2008.

Dominican Nuns of Our Lady of Perpetual Help Home. *A Memoir of Mary Ann.*

Escrivá de Balaguer, José Maria. *The Way.* New York: Scepter, 1992.

Kreeft, Peter. *Making Sense of Suffering.* Cincinnati: Servant Books, 1986.

Lewis, C. S. *The Problem of Pain.* New York: HarperCollins, 2001.

Yancey, Philip. *Where is God When it Hurts.* Grand Rapids, MI: Zondervan, 1997.

Websites

Barron, Bishop Robert. "Stephen Fry, Job, and Suffering." *Word on Fire* video, 10:07. Posted February 26, 2015. http://www.wordonfire.org/resources/video/stephen-fry-job-and-suffering/4671/.

Falasca, Stefania. "The little letters of 'Nennolina,'" *30Days* (May 2010): http://www.30giorni.it/articoli_id_22702_13.htm.

Letters of Antonietta Meo: http://john114.org/Antonietta/Summary.htm.

Pope John Paul II. *Salvifici Doloris.* Vatican City: Libreria Editrice Vaticana, 1984. http://w2.vatican.va/content/john-paul-ii/en/

apost_letters/1984/documents/hf_jp-ii_apl_11021984_salvifici-doloris.html.

"Stephen Fry – On God." YouTube video, 2:15. Posted by "Sam Olawale," October 7, 2015. https://www.youtube.com/watch?v=B5RtDpva7nE.